# Study Guide

## *for*

# Gardner's Art through the Ages: The Western Perspective
## Volume II
### Twelfth Edition

Fred S. Kleiner
Christin J. Mamiya

*Prepared by*
Kathleen Cohen
*San Jose State University*

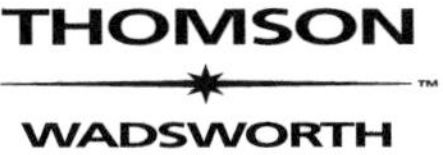


AUSTRALIA · CANADA · MEXICO · SINGAPORE · SPAIN · UNITED KINGDOM · UNITED STATES

ISBN: 0-495-00662-9



**Thomson Higher Education**
**10 Davis Drive**
**Belmont, CA 94002-3098**
**USA**

**Asia**
Thomson Learning
5 Shenton Way #01-01
UIC Building
Singapore 068808

**Australia/New Zealand**
Thomson Learning
102 Dodds Street
Southbank, Victoria 3006
Australia

**Canada**
Nelson
1120 Birchmount Road
Toronto, Ontario M1K 5G4
Canada

**Europe/Middle East/South Africa**
Thomson Learning
High Holborn House
50/51 Bedford Row
London WC1R 4LR
United Kingdom

**Latin America**
Thomson Learning
Seneca, 53
Colonia Polanco
11560 Mexico D.F.
Mexico

**Spain/Portugal**
Paraninfo
Calle/Magallanes, 25
28015 Madrid, Spain

# Contents

# Preface

This study guide accompanies the 12th edition of *Gardner's Art through the Ages: The Western Perspective* and is intended to help you assimilate the information that you will encounter as you read the text. The study guide contains the following exercises which will enable you to organize and learn the material presented in your art history course:

SHORT ANSWER QUESTIONS: These questions emphasize the basic terminology of art history, important historical individuals, and mythological figures, and important concepts, places, and dates. While many of these questions are factual, others ask you to list stylistic characteristics of particular works or to write the meanings attributed to particular works and to set them within their historical contexts.

DISCUSSION QUESTIONS: Each unit ends with a variety of discussion questions that will help you assess the significance of what you have learned. Some questions are of a general, philosophical nature, requiring reference to specific artists and styles. Some ask for interpretation of theories, sometimes with reference to your daily experience. Others involve the comparison of works, artists, and styles from different times and places. These are calculated to broaden your perspective by asking you to see familiar styles in unfamiliar contexts.

SUMMARY CHARTS: Summary charts are organized chronologically and contain sections for you to fill in with names of major artistic movements or artists, typical examples, stylistic characteristics, and relevant historical information.

SELF-QUIZZES: Self-quizzes appear at the end of the study guide and each one covers multiple chapters of the text. Each quiz contains several images that you have not seen before. You are asked to attribute them to a particular artist or period and give the reasons for your attribution. Answers are given at the back, so that you can determine for yourself how well you are progressing.

If you read the text and complete the exercises in the study guide, by the end of the course you should be able to do the following:

1. Define and use common art historical terms.
2. Identify time periods, geographic centers, and stylistic characteristics of major art movements.
3. Identify significant religious concepts, philosophical movements, historical figures, events, and places and discuss their relationship to works of art.
4. Recognize and discuss the iconography popular during various historical periods, as well as the iconography of specific works of art.
5. Set art works in their historical context, comparing and contrasting the reasons why various cultures created works of art as well as the formal characteristics that identify them.
6. Discuss the work of major artists in terms of their artistic concerns and stylistic characteristics, the media they used, and the principal influences upon them.

7. Attribute unfamiliar works of art to particular artists, historical periods, countries, and/or styles.

Many of the questions in the guide will serve as excellent preparation for examinations. Instructors may wish to base some of their examination questions on the materials covered in the guide; they may even wish to establish with students at the beginning of the course that a specified percentage of the examination questions will be taken from the guide.

-Kathleen Cohen, Professor of Art History<br>
San Jose State University

# Tips on Becoming a Successful Student

You are starting on an art historical adventure that will enrich your lives. Some of you may pursue additional studies in art history, but for others, this may be the only art history course that you will you take. Whichever path you choose, this course will open the past through objects of beauty created by men and women from many cultures. You may want to visit the sites of the magnificent buildings you have studied as well as the objects—both familiar and new—housed in museums. These visits will continue to enrich your life.

 Your instructor's lectures, the textbook, and the Study Guide all reinforce each other. As you proceed in this course you will learn new study techniques that will further enhance your learning. The section below outlines a number of strategies that successful students use. Try them out and see which work best for you.

**ACTIVELY LISTENING TO LECTURES:**
During your professor's lectures you will have the opportunity to see large projected images of beautiful works of art, to hear when and why they were created, and to learn what they meant to the people for whom they were made. Your professor's lectures are extremely important both in learning the material and in discovering what he or she feels is most important for you to learn. Pay careful attention to the course syllabus, checking to see the order in which topics will be covered, for you will find that you get more out of the lectures if you have read the relevant material in your text book before coming to class.

It is very important to learn how to keep your mind focused on what the instructor is saying and not succumb to the darkness that surrounds you or to let your mind wander. Taking notes on what the lecturer is saying as well as drawing sketches of the projected art works not only imprints the material in your mind, but also helps to keep your mind focused.

You should start with a general title for the lecture and the date. Good students create a different paragraph for each work the teacher presents, headed by the artist, the title and the date. If it is a work of architecture, they include the location. On the left leave a space to draw a simple sketch. It need not be elaborate or even competent, but will serve to help you visualize the work. Then write down a few phrases that the teacher says about the significance of the work and its stylistic characteristics. You should underline the information that the instructor emphasizes.

When you look at your notes in the light, you may find that they are sloppy and hard to read, but nevertheless they are important. Rewriting them after class will further imprint the information in your mind and will provide you with material for integrating into your summary charts as you prepare for examinations. You should star the works from the lecture that also appear in the text, for you will probably want to focus your study on these works.

Sample Lecture notes:
**S Apollinare Nuovo, Ravenna. c. 504  6th c  Early Byzantine.

Theodoric patron. 3 aisle basilica form w/arcade. raised beam. wood ceiling, Mosaics above arcade & windows. Processions; prophets Christ life; beardless Christ wears purple. Flattened figures; gold background.

The abbreviated notes above will tell you that the teacher is most interested in your recognizing the work as Early Byzantine, done in the 6th century, that it is a basilica with an arcade (later you might look up arcade and define it if you don't know). It is decorated mosaics with processions and scenes from Christ's life. Gold backgrounds are typical and the figures are somewhat flattened.  You have also noted by the two stars that the book is illustrated in the text. As you can see, the sketch is rudimentary, but it will help recall the image to your mind. (I should confess that when I was an undergraduate, my painting teacher said "If you have to paint, do, but if you can do anything else, do that!" Needless to say, I was crushed, but I think I have been a better art historian than I would have been a painter.) The point is, you don't have to be an artist to make little sketches of the works shown in class, and they will help you learn. You might want to leave a space after each image in your lecture notes to incorporate specific information from the text book.

**READING THE TEXT:**
The text will reinforce the instructor's lectures and provide additional background in many areas. Whenever you run across a term that you don't understand, either in the reading or the lectures, look it up in the glossary in the back of the book. You can use the glossary to check spelling and pronunciation. You can find a guide to the pronunciation of artist's names on the website at http://art.wadsworth.com/gardnerwestern12. The notes and bibliography for each chapter provide excellent resources for assembling your bibliography for a research assignment. Each chapter contains a map at the beginning and a chronology at the end. Use these as resources when you are filling out the Study Guide.

**FILLING OUT THE STUDY GUIDE:**
The Study Guide provides the place to write and to synthesize. Filling out the exercises in the Study Guide will contribute a great deal to your success in

mastering the class material. Research has shown that the act of writing down a fact or idea rather than merely reading it serves to imprint it more securely in your mind. Furthermore, reading through the text for specific answers will help you concentrate. With the exception of the lists of definitions or identifications at the beginning of each section and the Discussion Questions at the end of each chapter, the questions follow the order of the text, so keep your study guide beside you as you read. Fill out these questions as you read though your text and use both its glossary and index to find any terms that you may have missed as well as the terms and names found in the Definition/Identification questions.

You can use the text or sketches you made from your instructor's lectures as the basis for the sketches requested in the guide. Don't worry if your sketches are awkward; it is the idea that counts. It is also important to know that most people have better visual than verbal memories, and you are more apt to retain the image from your little sketches than from a written description. The maps are another type of visual shorthand, and they will help you put the art works in context and see which works are most closely related geographically. Use the maps in your text to locate the sites requested in the guide.

**ABOUT LEARNING DATES:**
Students tend to be most apprehensive about how many dates they are expected to learn. Some instructors put much greater emphasis on learning dates than do others. My recommendation is to learn a structure for dates—patterns–rather than trying to memorize many individual dates. The guide asks you to complete a chronology for various sections. The request to write dates in the guide is to help you organize a structure, to create a scaffolding on which you can hang events, art styles, and artists. We learn patterns better than isolated facts, and it becomes easier and easier to connect facts once you have established the chronological structure, the basic pattern.

You should not attempt to memorize all the dates for the various periods, but the mere act of writing them down will help you create your mental structure. For the early periods think in terms of millennia, for later materials in terms of centuries, and for recent materials you might want to think in terms of quarter centuries. Often you need to learn only a few significant dates, and then organize various materials either around that date, before or after it. You will not be too far off you know that the High Renaissance was roughly the first quarter of the 16th century, with Leonardo starting work a bit earlier and Michelangelo continuing to work later. Sometimes a particular artistic event can help you determine the approximate date of an art work: two that come to mind are the invention of contrapposto in Greece in the early 5th century BCE and of linear perspective in Italy about 1425. Works that contain those characteristics must therefore be after the relevant date. You can often build from what you know to what you don't know if you think and ask yourself questions rather than just trying to memorize a series of dates.

**THE DISCUSSION QUESTIONS:**
The discussion questions at the end of each chapter are more comprehensive than the more factual questions included earlier, and they are designed to help you integrate what you have learned, make comparisons between the arts of different periods and places, and to speculate about explanations and theories. Your instructor may use them as the basis of discussion in your class, or you may discuss them with students in your study group (see Establishing a Study Group below). You may also use them as the basis for practice in writing essays (see below).

**ESTABLISHING A STUDY GROUP:**
Research has shown that students who work with others in study groups generally do better than students who work by themselves. The three elements that you will need to coordinate are 1) locating two to three students who would like to join your group, 2) finding a convenient time and 3) finding a convenient place to get together. If you live on campus in a dormitory 2 and 3 will be easier, but even if yours is essentially a commuting campus you can usually find a quiet place and a convenient time to get together in one of the classrooms that is not in use or in a corner of the student cafeteria. Some students like to get together for an hour before class each week, while others prefer to spend an evening every week or every two weeks. You instructor will probably give you a minute or two at the end of class to identify other students who might be interested in forming a group with you or groups of their own.

Activities at group meetings can vary. The discussion questions in the study guide can serve as an excellent focus for your group, with different students assigned to prepare to lead the group in discussion of specific questions each week. Each student might be responsible for preparing a specific number of image cards that can be used by the group to quiz each other.

**SUMMARY CHARTS:**
Among the most important aspects of the Study Guide are the Summary Charts included throughout the guide. It is here that you integrate the various things that you have learned from the lectures, your reading of the text, films you have seen, the *ArtStudy* CD-ROM and Internet exercises, and the work you have done in the guide itself. As I noted above, we remember patterns much better than individual items, and filling out the Summary Charts creates patterns in your

head as well as on paper, for the activity forces you to organize and relate things to each other. Filling out the Chronology Charts as well as the map sections will help you understand how works of art relate to each other in both time and space. And actively filing in the chart is much more effective than merely reading a summary that someone else has prepared. You will probably find this method of studying so effective that you will create your own summary charts for other courses.

**STUDYING FOR EXAMINATIONS:**
The self-quizzes included in the Study Guide can be a great help in preparing you for course examinations as well as in letting you know how well you are progressing. The quizzes include types of questions often asked in art history examinations: multiple choice, chronology exercises, short answer and essay questions, and attribution of unknown images. The guide itself contains fill-ins, short answer, definitions, and essay questions. If you fill out the Study Guide as you go along and fill out the summary sheets and take the self-quizzes included in each section before examinations, you will find that you will not need to "cram" the night before. While "cramming" can put things into short-term memory, it is not an effective way to learn. The various exercises done over an extended period of time put things into your long-term memory where they have a much better chance of being retained. The best students study as they go along; they will have completed their review and might go to a movie on the night before the examination while their classmates are staying up all night trying to re-read the text and make out the scribblings in their lecture notes.

**CREATING YOUR OWN CHARTS, REVIEWING IMAGES, & CREATING FLASH CARDS:**
You might wish to create a master sheet that includes all the images from your lectures as well as others from the text book that relate to your instructor's lectures, following the model that I introduced in the section about taking notes. You could write out or, better yet, put it on a computer so you can make additions as you run across new material you want to incorporate. If you are using a laptop, you might wish to make your class notes directly on the computer, again using abbreviations as you listen to the teacher's lecture, and then fill in additional information afterward. Some students like to look up images on the web and download them into their computer notes. The *ArtStudy* CD-ROM that came with your textbook contains various images from each chapter of the text, and you might be able to locate others by looking up the artist or the work on the web using Google or going to sources like http://worldart.sjsu.edu. Bringing all of these things together as you create your charts will be a very effective way to study for examinations.

Active involvement with the images themselves by creating image flash cards is an excellent way to review the visual images. Some instructors mount slides in lighted cases while others create web sites with review images. Both of these are useful techniques. However, you can create your own image review using the *ArtStudy* CD-ROM as it allows you to create flashcard groups of all the images available. One final method is to use Xeroxes of the images in the text, mounting them on 4 x 5 cards, and putting the relevant information on the opposite side. Both flashcard methods allow you to sorting them by style, by chronology, or by medium. You might work with another student, selecting examples to test each other. Any devices that you can use to engage actively with the material will help you learn!

**ADDITIONAL RESOURCES:**
The publishers of the text have prepared additional resources that will help you learn.

The *ArtStudy* CD-ROM that came with your textbook is an excellent source which I recommend to you. The interactive the maps and the timelines are fun as well as instructive, for you get to drag and drop site names and art works into their appropriate slots. A number of the chapters have excellent sections on Architectural basics, clearly explaining the principles and giving you a drag-and-drop quiz that can test how well you have learned the principles.   There are Internet activities that are linked to websites with images that you can compare, analyze, or just find out about. The On-line Quizzes are excellent and will be important ways to study for examinations.

The publishers have developed a website for the textbook that includes exercises, quizzes, flashcards of chapter terms with pronunciation, timelines and maps. Its URL is http://art.wadsworth.com/gardnerwestern12.

**TAKING THE EXAM:**
It is important to be calm when you take the exam. This means checking the date and time of the examination and getting there a little early so that you have a chance to relax before the exam begins. It also means being sure that you have the appropriate type of answer sheet, if one is needed, a sharpened pencil for marking it, appropriate paper for writing an essay, and a pen, as well as backups in case the pencil breaks or the pen runs out of ink. Some of these things may seem trivial, but if you are not prepared, you can be thrown off base. Before you begin, write your name clearly on all your examination materials, including the answer sheet and the various pages you used to write your essay. There is invariably one student who forgets to write his or her name on something of importance.

Find out if the instructor subtracts for wrong answers or just counts up correct answers. Some instructors do not want you to guess, but others don't care. I always tell students to guess rather than leaving something blank. Your wrong answer may be quite creative and cheer the instructor up. (I still recall the student who identified a Renaissance floor plan as a Mondrian painting!) Whatever you do, read the questions carefully. Also read the DIRECTIONS carefully. I always allow students to select one essay question out of three or four, but every so often there is some poor soul who tries to answer them all, and does them all badly. When you have finished the examination, check to make sure that you have correctly transferred all your answers to the mechanically scored answer sheet, if you have used one as part of your examination, and that all the blanks are filled in. Check again that your name is on everything, turn in your papers, and go home and relax.

**WRITING ESSAYS:**
Learning how to write clearly and succinctly is one of the most important tasks of your college career, no matter what your major. While some examination questions will be multiple choice, fill in or short answer, most exams will also include at least one essay question. Since many essay questions will either ask you to trace the development of an art form, to compare and contrast the work of two cultures or two artists, or to set particular works within their cultural contexts, the work that you do in your study guide will prepare you to answer them. The summary charts are particularly useful in this regard, for as you fill them out you do the type of summary and synthesis that serves as the basis for answers to many essay questions. Many of the discussion questions in the guide are similar to essay questions that you will find in examinations. The materials you wrote in the summary charts can be extremely useful, for you are asked to list typical examples of the work of each period or artist. Here are the examples you need for your essay. You will most likely be able to include the material you write in the stylistic characteristics column. Look carefully at the essays included to the answers to the identifications in the self-quizzes at the end of each section of the study guide. You will see how specific examples are cited in the context of generalizations and how both stylistic features and iconography are used to provide attributions to specific cultures and/or artists. For many essays the material that you included in the significant historical people, events and ideas will be highly relevant.

You can practice writing essays by using some of the questions in the guide. First of all, read the question carefully and answer the question that is asked. This is important, for often students will go off on a tangent and not clearly deal with what they are asked. With many questions you are asked to support your generalizations by specific examples. Be sure and do so! It might be helpful to set some time limits for your practice essays so that you can get an idea of how much you will be able to write in 15 minutes or in 30. You could work with members of your study group, perhaps by all tackling the same essay. At the end of a set time you could critique each other's essays, pointing out good points and offering suggestions.

Whatever essay question that you are tackling, first jot down your ideas and then make an outline of your proposed answer, noting which specific examples you will use to support the points you are making. The outline will serve at least two purposes: 1) to organize your thinking and to help you build you essay to answer the question that you were asked, and 2) to let the reader know what points you would have made in case you run out of time. Begin your essay with an introduction noting the subject of your essay. Develop the points that you made in your outline, and then end with an appropriate conclusion. Assume that you are writing for an uninformed reader. Don't omit relevant information because you think that the teacher already knows it; your instructor is interested in what you know, so be sure and make that clear.

One last tip: Even if you are thrown by the questions, don't just walk out and leave a blank paper. Write something!! You may not gain any points, but you won't be any worse off, and you might just come up with something that is worth a point or two.

**VISITING A MUSEUM AND ANALYSING A WORK OF ART:**
If you are anywhere near a museum, your instructor will probably urge you to visit it and to study and write about one or more works of art you see there. No matter how good a reproduction you can find in your text or on the CD or web, experiencing a real work of art is a different experience, and it is one that your instructor is preparing you for.  The first thing that will strike you is the scale of the work; objects that appeared to be the same size in 35mm slides may be only a few inches tall while others may be over 40 feet high.

After you have walked though the collection, select the work you want to write about and look at it very very carefully. If it is a piece of sculpture walk all around it and if it is a painting or graphic go up close to it and look at the brushstrokes or other marks. Purchase a postcard of the work or make a photograph of it if photography is permitted.  There are many different ways to analyze works of art, but here is one scheme which you might want to use.

1.  Write down the museum you are visiting, then the name of the work, the artist who created it, the date, the place where it was made, and the size. What technique and what materials did the artist use?

2.   Write down why you selected that particular work of art? What made it attractive to you? What sort of emotional reaction did you have to the work?

3.   Next describe the subject matter. What is actually represented? I s the work a portrait, a still life, a landscape? Is it a religious or mythological image? Is it telling a story? If so, what is the source of the story? Are there any symbols in the work? What do they mean? What do you think the work meant to the people who created the work?

4.   Analyze the formal elements of the work using the terms that you will find later in this chapter: form and composition, line, texture, mass and volume. Study the color, describing the hues the artist used, the value, saturation and intensity of the hues, and whether the artist emphasized contrasting colors or colors that were very close to each other. Consider how the artist organized the forms: the so-called design principles of balance, rhythm, proportion, etc. Is there a focal point or do the forms seem randomly placed?  Do diagonal lines or verticals and horizontals dominate? Do the forms seem smooth or jagged, regular or irregular, symmetrical or asymmetrical, dynamic or static? Do the forms seem to stay on the surface or recede into the picture space? Is the space shallow or deep? Did the artist use perspective and foreshortening to create recession?

5.   Last consider how effectively the artist used the materials and the formal elements to create a particular impression or to illustrate the theme of the work. How successful do you think the artist was?

**TIPS ON WRITING A RESEARCH PAPER**

You may be asked to do a research paper, a paper in which you will go into greater depth about a theme or the work of a particular of a particular artist. You will be using a variety of materials written by different scholars either in journals or in books, and you will use your local library as well as on-line sources to locate these materials.

Your instructor may suggest a guide to writing about art which will explain how to go about writing the paper itself and which will explain how to avoid plagiarizing your sources. Your instructor may also have a particular form that he or she wishes you to follow in footnoting your sources and creating your bibliography. Most art historians use the form approved by the College Art Association, which you can find at http://www.collegeart.org/caa/publications/AB/ABStyleGuide.html. The style guide is very thorough, covering capitalization, hyphenation and many other details, but of greatest importance for you are the sections containing the appropriate forms to use for quotations, footnotes and bibliographies.

And now it is time to begin your reading of the textbook. Scan the questions below before you start your reading, and then answer the questions and fill in the blanks as appropriate.

# Introduction to Volume II

# REVIEW OF THE SUBJECTS AND VOCABULARY OF ART HISTORY*

**TEXT PAGES  xvii-xxxi**

If you did the Study Guide for Volume I of the text, you will already have defined most of the following terms. You might want to review them there.  If you are only working with Volume II, be sure that you fill out the sections below because you will need the terminology as you proceed.

**TERMINOLOGY REVIEW**
Use the text and the glossary or go online to find the meaning of the terms as used by art historians and define them in below.

form:

composition:

medium (pl. media):

technique:

hue:

value or tonality:


intensity or saturation:


space:


mass: (The term is not in the glossary, so I will put in the definition for you).
Mass defines a three-dimensional volume in space.

line: (The term is not in the glossary, so I will put in the definition for you) A
series of points moving in space, as contrasted with the use of mass or shape
forms. Lines may be thin or thick. A contour line defines the outer shape of an
object.

## ICONOGRAPHIC REVIEW

1.  Identify the role played by each of the following Greek gods and goddesses, and
    indicate their Roman equivalents.

    Aphrodite


    Apollo


    Ares


    Artemis


    Athena

Demeter

Eros

Hades

Hera

Hermes

Poseidon

Zeus

2.  Briefly define the following Buddhist terms:

Amitaba (Amida)

Bodhisattva

Buddha

Mahayana

Mudra

Therevada (Hinayana)

3.  Briefly define the following Hindu terms:

Devi

Linga

Samsara

Siva

Vishnu

4.  List six events from Christ's incarnation and childhood that are commonly
    portrayed in art:
    a.                      b.                      c.

    d.                      e.                      f.

    List six events from his public ministry that are commonly portrayed in art:
    a.                      b.                      c.

    d.                      e.                      f.

    What is mean by Christ's Passion?

    List twelve events from the Passion that are commonly portrayed in art:

    a.                      b.                      c.

    d.                      e.                      f.

    g.                      h.                      i.

    j.                      k.                      l.

**ARCHITECTURAL REVIEW**
Using the text and the glossary, define the following terms as they apply to
architecture. You may draw diagrams if you prefer.

plan


section


elevation


entablature


engaged column


voussoir


keystone


barrel vault


groin vault


rib vault


dome


pendentive

nave

transept

apse

ambulatory

arcade

clerestory

# FROM GOTHIC TO RENAISSANCE
## FOURTEENTH CENTURY ITALIAN ART

**TEXT PAGES 400-423**

**THE CITY STATES/ POLITICS AND ECONOMICS**
Name four Italian city states that were very successful commercially during the late Gothic period:

a.                                         b.

c.                                         d.

**DISTRUPTION AND CHANGE/ LETTERS AND LEARNING**
1.  What was the Black Death and what effect did it have on art?


2.  What was Humanism and how did it affect art?


**THE MOVEMENT AWAY FROM MEDIEVALISM IN ART**
1.  Which style dominated Medieval Italian painting?

List three of its stylistic characteristics.

a.

b.

c.

2.  Who was St. Francis?


List three episodes of his life that are illustrated in Berlingieri's altarpiece (FIG. 14-1).

a.

b.

c.

3. Identify two trends shown in the works of Nicola and Giovanni Pisano that later become significant in the development of Renaissance art.

a.

b.

4. Although Cimabue was deeply influenced by the Italo-Byzantine style, he moved beyond it in the following ways:

a.

b.

5. What seems to have been the artistic traditions that influenced Giotto and contributed to the shaping of his style?

6. List two characteristics of Giotto's style as seen by comparing his *Madonna Enthroned* (FIG. 14-7) with Cimabue's version of the same subject (FIG. 14-6).

a.

b.

7. Giotto created a great fresco cycle in the _________________chapel in

_____________. It was consecrated in the year_________. The subjects of the framed scenes deal with:

8. List four characteristics of Giotto's style as seen in the Lamentation scene (FIG. 14-9).

a.

b.

c.

d.

9.  What is the difference between "true fresco" and "fresco secco"?

10. The subject of Duccio's *Maesta Altarpiece* (FIGS. 14-10 and 14-11) was :

    List three stylistic elements he derived from the Byzantine tradition:

    a.

    b.

    c.

    List three ways in which he modified it:

    a.

    b.

    c.

11. How did Simone Martini help to form the so-called International style?

    List four characteristics of that style.

    a.

    b.

    c.

    d.

12. Panoramic views of the city of Siena and its surrounding countryside
    were painted by ____________________in the Palazzo Pubblico in Siena
    as part of a fresco known as ____________________________.

    What revolutionary aspects are found in this fresco (FIGS. 14-15 and 14-16)?

13. How were artists trained in Italy during the 14th and 15th centuries?

14. What historical event seems to be the subject of *The Triumph of Death* (FIG. 14-21)?


## DISCUSSION QUESTIONS

1. Discuss the effects of social and economic changes between the late thirteenth and late fourteenth centuries on Italian art of the period.

2. If you have Volume I of the text, compare the versions of the *Nativity* by Nicola and Giovanni Pisano (FIGS. 14-3 and 14-4) with the Late Antique *Ludovisi Battle Sarcophagus* (FIG. 7-71). How are the Pisani works similar to this Roman example? How are they different from it and from each other?

3. Compare Duccio's *Betrayal of Jesus* (FIG. 14-11) with another painting in this chapter; note particularly the use of space, three-dimensional volume, and the sense of drama.

4. If you have Volume I of the text, compare Simone Martini's *Annunciation* (FIG. 14-12) with the *Virgin of Jeanne d'Evreux* (FIG. 13-35). Can you find any stylistic characteristics of the French figure that can be related to those of Simone's version? Discuss the historical factors that account for the French influence in his work.

5. Discuss Florence Cathedral (FIGS 14-17 and 14-18), noting especially the way in which decorative details are integrated with the construction as a whole. Does Florence Cathedral share and design features with other cathedrals?

## LOOKING CAREFULLY, DESCRIBING AND ANALYZING

Look carefully at Lorenzetti's *Effects of Good Government* in the city and in the country (FIGS. 14-15 and 14-16) and compare them to the landscape and architectural scenes in on Berlinghieri's *St. Francis* altarpiece (FIG. 14-1). Write a one page essay analyzing each of the images using the following terms: form and composition; material and technique; space, mass and volume, line, and color. Here are some questions that might help you with your analysis, but do not be limited by them. What differences do you see in the artists' approaches to composition and form, particularly in the depiction of space? How does each artist describe architectural forms and the forms of the mountains? In each case how are human figures related to the environment both in scale and position. Which has the greatest sense of space? Which elements contribute to that sense?

# MAP

Circle the following on the map below.

Siena          Florence               Pisa                    Milan

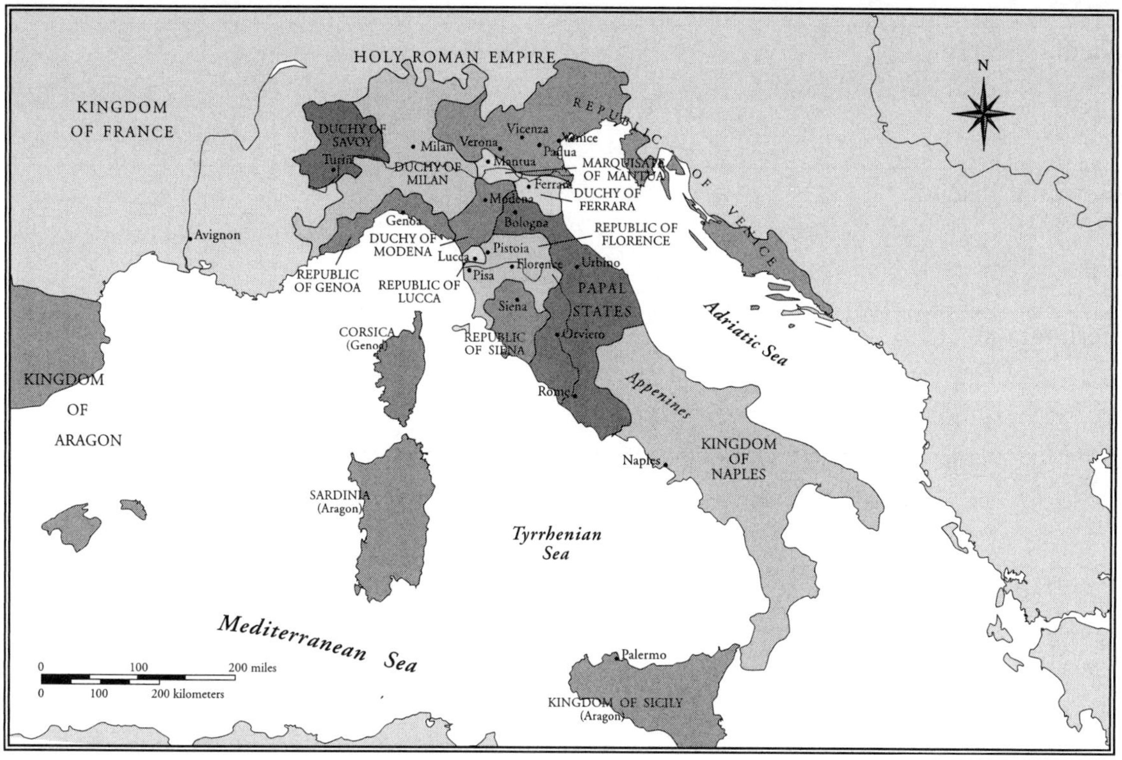

**MAP 14-1** Italy around 1400

SUMMARY OF LATE GOTHIC ARTISTS IN ITALY

Fill in the following charts as much as possible from memory, then check your answers against the text in Chapter 14.

| | Typical Examples | Stylistic Characteristics |
| --- | --- | --- |
| Nicola Pisano | | |
| Giovanni Pisano | | |
| Berlinghieri | | |
| Duccio | | |
| Cavallini & Cimabue | | |
| Giotto | | |
| Simoni Martini | | |
| Lorenzetti | | |

# 15

# PIETY, PASSION, AND POLITICS
## FIFTEENTH-CENTURY ART IN NORTHERN EUROPE AND SPAIN

**TEXT PAGES 424-451**

List two factors that contributed to the development of cities in the fifteenth century:

a.                                        b.

**FRENCH MANUSCRIPT ILLUMINATION**
1. What is a Book of Hours?


2. Name the artists who illuminated the *Trés Riches Heures du Duc de Berry* shown in FIGS 15-1 and 15-2:

3. Describe the stylistic characteristics that link the illuminations done by the Limbourg brothers with fourteenth-century Sienese painting:
   a.

   b.

   c.

   d.

**15TH CENTURY FLEMISH ART**
1. Name two northern dukes who are generally considered to have been the greatest patrons of the arts in northern Europe in the late fourteenth and early fifteenth centuries:

a.                                        b.

2.  What was the symbolic meaning of the *Well of Moses* at the Chartresuse de Champmol (FIG. 15-3)?

3.  What new feature is seen in Broderlam's wings from the *Retable de Champmol* (FIG. 15-4)?

    Name two medieval conventions he retains:
    a.

    b.

4.  Define the following terms:

    polyptych

    retable

    triptych

5.  What is the general theme of the *Ghent Altarpiece* (FIGS. 15-5 and 15-6)?

    Write the subjects of the various panels in the corresponding spaces below:

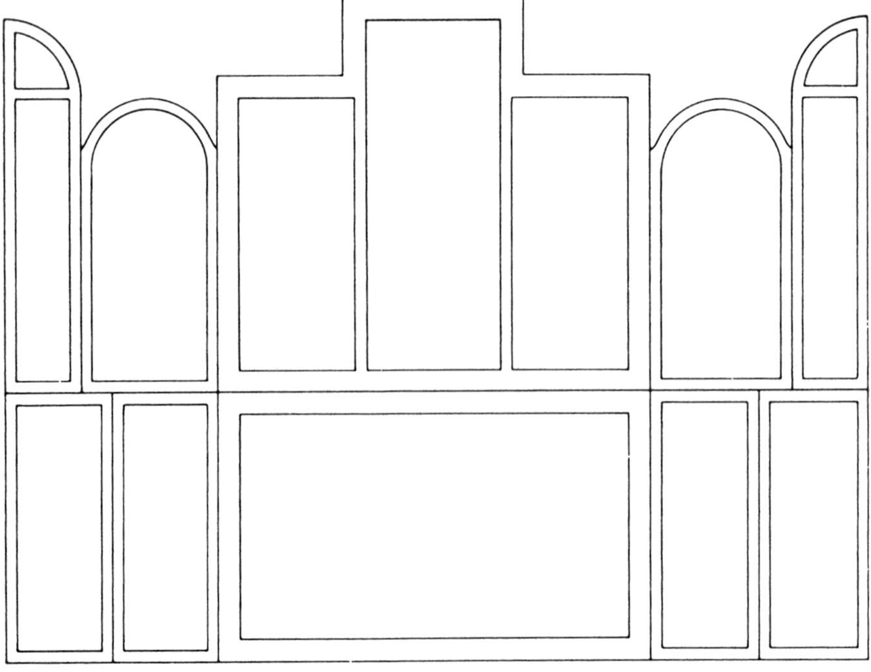

What is symbolized by the following groups on the lower wings?

hermits: _____________________ judges: _____________________

pilgrims: _____________________ knights: _____________________

6. What painting technique was perfected by fifteenth-century Flemish painters?


Briefly describe the technique:


In what respects did it prove superior to the tempera technique?


7. In contrast to the complex symbolism of Jan van Eyck, what did Rogier van der Weyden stress in his paintings?


List three characteristics of his style:

a.

b.

c.

8. Describe the role played by the Guild of Saint Luke in the life of the northern painters in the fifteenth century and the way in which a young man attained membership in the guild:


9. How did most women artists receive their training during the fifteenth and sixteenth centuries?

10. Name the two fifteenth-century Flemish painters who demonstrated the greatest interest in the depiction of space and cubic form.

a.                                          b.

11. Scholars believe that _______________________ was the first northern artist to utilize a single vanishing point for construction of an architectural interior.

12. What is the symbolic meaning of the following items in the central panel of the Portinari Altarpiece (FIG. 15-10)?

Iris and columbine:

Sheaf of wheat:

Harp of David:

13. In what sort of subject matter did Hans Memling specialize?

Briefly describe his style:

14. List two factors that contributed to the great demand for images for private devotion:

a.

b.

15. What effect did the blending of sacred and secular have upon the way devotional images were painted?

16. Who was the Master of Flémalle?

List three characteristics of his style:

a.

b.

c.

17. What do the book, candle, water jug and towels symbolize in the *Mérode Altarpiece* (FIG. 15-12)?

18. What is the probable purpose of the painting *Giovanni Arnolfini and His Bride* (FIG. 15-13)?

   List four symbols contained in the painting and give their meanings:

   a.

   b.

   c.

   d.

19. What is the setting of Christus' painting that is identified with the legend of Saint Eligius (FIG. 15-15)?

   Who might have commissioned it?

20. What is new and significant about the pose of the *Man in a Red Turban* (FIG. 15-16)?

21. List the Flemish characteristics of Rogier's *Portrait of a Lady* (FIG. 15-17) that distinguish it from the work of Italian artists such as Ghirlandaio (FIG. 16-31)

   a.

   b.

   c.

22. What are the primary subjects of the panels of Bosch's *Garden of Earthly Delights* (FIG. 15-18)?

Left:

Center:

Right:

Exterior:

**15th-CENTURY FRENCH ART**
List two features of Fouquet's panel (FIG. 15-19) that are similar to Flemish donor portraits:
    a.

    b.

**15th-CENTURY GERMAN ART**
1. Name two groups of people who were the primary patrons in fifteenth-century Germany:

    a.                            b.

2. Describe the stylistic features that differentiate Lochner's version of the *Madonna in the Rose Garden* (FIG. 15-20) with Giotto's *Madonna Enthroned* (FIG. 14-7).

3. List three characteristics of the style of Konrad Witz:

    a.

    b.

    c.

4. What subject did Stoss depict in the center of the Krakow altarpiece (FIG. 15-22)?

List three typical Late Gothic characteristics of his style:

a.

b.

c.

5.  What mood is most typically expressed in the figures carved by Riemenschneider  (FIG. 15-23)?


6.  Define the following terms associated with graphics:

burin


engraving


etching


intaglio


relief


woodcut

7.  What is the *Nuremberg Chronicle*?


What technique was used to produce it?

8.  In what medium did Martin Schongauer work?


Briefly characterize his style:

**15th-CENTURY SPANISH ART**
1. Name and describe the architectural style that was popular in Spain during the late 15th and 16th centuries:


## DISCUSSION QUESTIONS

1. Compare Sluter's figure of *Moses* (FIG. 15-3) with Donatello's *Saint Mark* (FIG. 16-7). In what way do the figures typify the concerns of northern and Italian artists.

2. Compare the treatment of the architecture and landscape in the work by the Limbourg Brothers (FIG. 15-2) with that in Ambrogio Lorenzetti's *Effects of Good Government* (FIG. 14-15 and 14-16). In what ways are they similar? In what ways do they differ?

3. Masaccio's *Holy Trinity* fresco (FIG. 16-12) and Campin's *Merode Altarpiece* (FIG. 15-12) were painted about the same time . Compare them from the point of view of scale, medium, and treatment of space. Does Campin use linear perspective? Identify the orthogonals in each and locate the vanishing point, if one exists. How do the two works reflect the different concerns of Italian and northern artists?

4. How does Jan van Eyck's approach to portraiture as shown in his self portrait (FIG. 15-16) differ from the approach of Italian portraitists, for example Botticelli's *Portrait of a Youth* (FIG. 16-28)?

5. Discuss the *Portinari Altarpiece* (FIG. 15-10) by Hugo van der Goes; note especially the iconography and the meaning of the disguised symbols. What stylistic influence do you see from Jan van Eyck? How does this altarpiece differ from Van Eyck's *Ghent Altarpiece* (FIG. 15-5 and 15-6)?

6. Compare Schongauer's *Saint Anthony* (FIG. 15-25) with Mantegna's representation of *Saint James* (FIG. 16-47) from the points of view of technique, meaning, and emotional impact. What stylistic devices were used to achieve the differing effects?

7. Compare Rogier van der Weyden's *Deposition* (FIG. 15-7) with a similar subject by Giotto (FIG. 14-9). Which moves you most? Why?

# LOOKING CAREFULLY, DESCRIBING AND ANALYZING

Look carefully at the *October* page by the Limbourg brothers from the *Tres Riches Heures du duc de Berry* shown on page 424 and in FIG. 15-2. Write at least one page analyzing the image, using the following terms: form and composition; material and technique; space, mass and volume, line, and color. Here are some questions that might help you with your analysis, but do not be limited by them. Describe each object that you see, starting from the bottom of the composition and going to the very top.  How do the artists approach the composition?  How do they divide the composition and how do they indicate that the space  is three dimensional? How do the artists describe architectural and natural forms? How are human figures related to the environment both in scale and position.

## MAP QUESTION

Circle the following on the map below:

Ghent          Bruges          Beaune          Cologne          Isenheim

Indicate the territory controlled by the Dukes of Burgundy in another color.

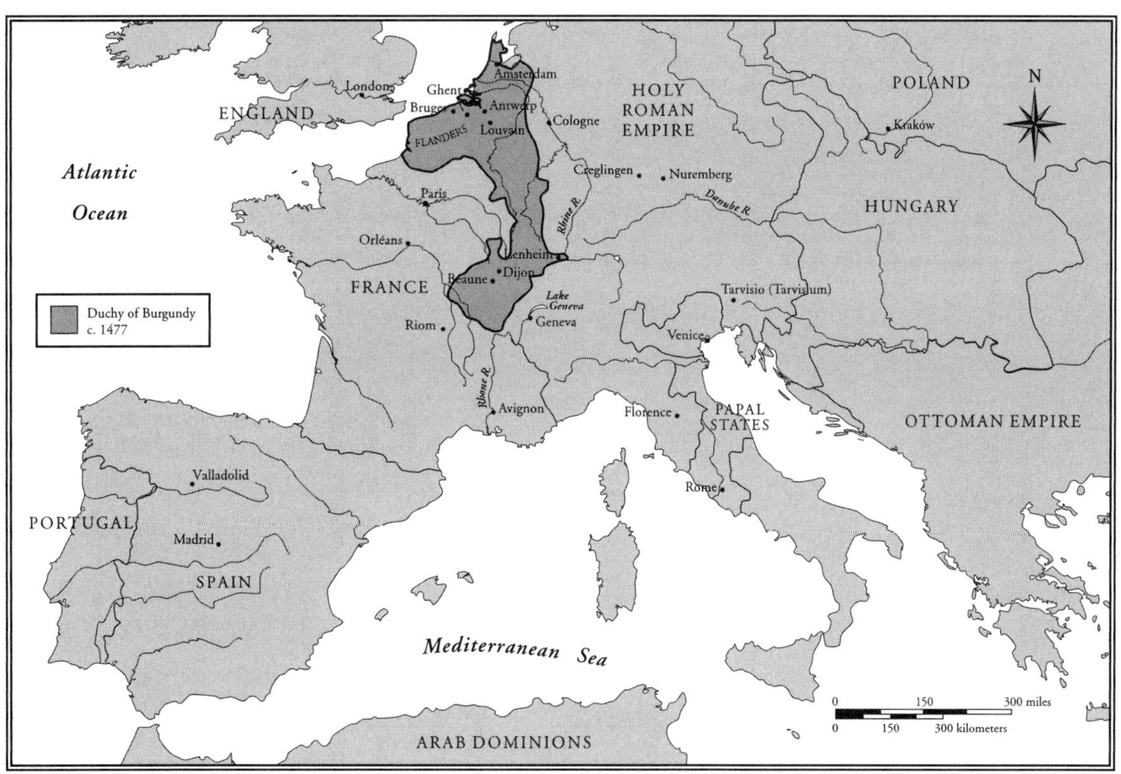


**MAP 15-1** Europe in the 15th century.

## SUMMARY OF FIFTEENTH-CENTURY NETHERLANDISH ARTISTS

Fill in the following charts as much as possible from memory, then check your answers against the text in Chapter 15.

|  | Typical Examples | Stylistic Characteristics |
| --- | --- | --- |
| Limbourg Brothers |  |  |
| Broederlam |  |  |
| Sluter |  |  |
| Campin |  |  |
| Jan van Eyck |  |  |
| Rogier van der Weyden |  |  |
| Bouts |  |  |
| Christus |  |  |
| van der Goes |  |  |
| Memling |  |  |
| Bosch |  |  |

# 16

# HUMANISM AND THE ALLURE OF ANTIQUITY
## FIFTEENTH-CENTURY ITALIAN ART

**TEXT PAGES  452-491**

1.  List three tenants that underlay Italian Humanism:

    a.

    b.

    c.

2.  What fifteenth-century German invention facilitated the distribution of books and the knowledge they contained?

3.  What was the basis of the wealth of the Medici family?

4.  List four roles played by the arts in fifteenth-century Italian princely courts.

    a.

    b.

    c.

    d.

**FLORENCE**

1. Name the two finalists for the commission of the north doors of the Baptistry of Florence and briefly describe their styles:

        Name                    Style

  a.

  b.

2. List three elements that constitute the greatness of Donatello's art,

  a.

  b.

  c.

3. Donatello's *Feast of Herod* (FIG. 16-3), done in 1425, marked the advent of

  ______________________.

4. The invention of linear prerspective is generally attributed to:

  _________________.

5. Define the following and draw and label a diagram if appropriate:

  Atmospheric perspective:

  Linear perspective:

  Orthogonals

Horizon line:


Vanishing point:


6. The artist who created the doors of the Baptistry of Florence Cathedral that best demonstrate the new principles of linear perspective was

___________________________.

What name did Michelangelo give to the doors?


7. Viewers identified saints from their symbolic attributes. Write the names of the following saints after the appropriate description: Augustine, Francis of Assisi, George, Jerome, Peter, Stephen.

Has a stigmata and wears a long robe, tied at the waist:

Young knight in armor with a cross on his shield, slaying a dragon:

Carries keys:

Scholar at his desk or a hermit in the wilderness:

Holds a stone:

Wears a bishop's vestments and mitre:

8. Name the patrons and the artists who created the following figures for Or San Michele:

<u>Artist</u>            <u>Patron</u>

*Saint George:* _______________________________________________

*Saint Mark:* _______________________________________________

*Quattro Santi Coronati:* _______________________________________
(4 crowned saints)

9.  In what figure did Donatello first utilize the principle of weight shift *(ponderation)?*

Describe *contrapposto*:

10. List three ways in which  Donatello's *Zuccone* (FIG. 16-8) differs strikingly from traditional representations of prophets:

a.

b.

c.

11. Gentile da Fabriano's *Adoration of the Magi* (FIG 16-9) is considered a masterpiece of the

_________________________________ style.

12. In contrast to Gentile's conservatism, Masaccio's *Tribute Money* (FIG. 16-10) was revolutionary. List three of his innovations:

a.

b.

c.

13. Although an artistic descendant of ___________________________, Masaccio used light to model his bulky figures in an entirely new way. Describe his method:

14. What two Renaissance interests are summed up in Masaccio's *Holy Trinity* fresco (FIG. 16-12)
a.

b.

15. Why did Brunelleschi design the dome of Florence Cathedral with an ogival rather than a semi-circular section?


16. Which of Brunelleschi's buildings most closely approximates the centralized plan?

Write down three phrases that describe its interior (FIG. 16-19):

a.

b.

c.

17. Who designed the Palazzo Medici-Riccardi (FIGS. 16-20, 16-21)?

The design of the courtyard shows the influence  of _______________.

What is rusticated stone and how was it used on the Palazzo Medici-Riccardi?


18. The Florentine artist who combined training in the International Style

with a passion for  perspective was___________________________.

19. What was the major significance of Donatello's bronze statue of *David* (FIG. 16-23)?

Describe the classical characteristics that are apparent in the figure:



It was commissioned for the courtyard of _____________________


20. One of the most important Italian sculptors of the second half of the fifteenth century, who was also a painter, was _________________.

How does his *David* (FIG. 16-24) differ from Donatello's version (FIG. 16-23)?

a.

b.

c.

21. List three adjectives that characterize the effect created by  Pollaiuolo's *Hercules and Antaeus* (FIG. 16-25):
a.

b.

c.

What seems to have been his primary artistic interest?

22. A literary source for Botticelli's *Birth of Venus*  (FIG. 16-27)  was

__________________, while a visual model was __________________.
Botticelli seems also to have been influenced by the allegorical pageants which appealed to his cultivated patrons.

List three characteristics of Botticelli's style.

a.

b.

c.

## THE RISE OF PORTRAITURE
1.  A  secularization of traditionally sacred themes can be seen in the portraits of Florentine women as represented in the fresco *The Birth of the Virgin* (FIG 16-32) by__________________.

2.  It has been said that the work of Ghirlandaio summed up the state of Florentine painting at the end of the fifteenth century.  List three of Ghirlandaio's achievements in painting:

a.


b.


c.


3. Italian cities commissioned portraits to commemorate famous
   condottieri. Two of the most famous are bronze equestrian figures.  List
   the condottieri, the artist, and the city:

   Condottieri                          Artist                    City

   ________________        ________________        ________________


   ________________        ________________        ________________


## FURTHER DEVELOPMENTS IN ARCHITECTURE

1. Three principles advocated by Leon Battista Alberti in his *De re aedificatoria*
   were:

   a.


   b.


   c.


2. What feature does the Palazzo Rucellai (FIG. 16-33) share with the
   Roman Colosseum?



   In what way is it markedly different?



3. Which Romanesque church seems to have influenced Alberti when he
   designed the facade of Santa Maria Novella (FIGS. 16-34, 16-35)?



   In what way did he modify the Romanesque original to create a highly
   sophisticated Renaissance design?

**IMAGES OF PIETY AND DEVOTION**

1.  The monk who painted a series of devotional frescos in the monastery

    of San Marco was:___________________.

    Briefly characterize his style:

2.  Under the influence of reliefs by Ghiberti and Donatello, Fra Filippo
    Lippi abandoned a style based on Masaccio's massive forms and
    developed his mature style, which is characterized by:

3.  The fifteenth-century sculptor _____________________,is best known
    for his production of glazed terra-cotta reliefs.

4.  What was the subject of  Perugino's fresco for the Sistine Chapel (FIG.
    16-40).

    What was its political significance?

    How does the work illustrate the principles of linear perspective?

**THE PRINCELY COURTS**

1.  List two projects commissioned by Ludovico Gonzaga in Mantua:

    a.                                b.

2.  The two Roman architectural motifs that Alberti locked together on the
    facade of Sant' Andrea in Mantua were:

    a.                                b.

    How does the plan of the church break with a centuries-old Christian
    building tradition?

3.  Explain the following terms with reference to Mantegna's Camera degli Sposi in Mantua (FIGS. 16-45 and 16-46):

trompe l'oeil


di sotto in su


4.  What two concerns did Mantegna integrate in his painting of the *Dead Christ* (FIG. 16-48):

a.

b.

5.  Piero della Francesca's great fresco cycle in San Francesco at
_____________________represents episodes from _________________.

List three characteristics  of Piero's style:

a.

b.

c.

6.  Piero's *Brera Altarpiece* (FIG. 16-50) was commissioned by ____________.
List two devices that Piero used to refer to his patron's dead wife:
a.

b.


**TURMOIL AT THE END OF THE CENTURY**
1.  What effect did the preaching of Savonarola have on the people of Florence?


2.  In what way could the frescos painted by Signorelli in Orvieto Cathedral (FIG. 16-51) be said to echo Savonarola's sermons?

The text describes Signorelli's "foreshortening." What does that mean?

## DISCUSSION QUESTIONS

1. If you have Volume I of the text, what degree of Classical influence is found in Nanni di Banco's *Quattro Santi Coronati* (FIG. 16-6) in comparison with earlier works by Nicola Pisano (FIG. 14-2) and the figures from Reims Cathedral (FIG. 13-22)? Note particularly the mastery of the contrapposto pose. In what way do Nanni di Banco's figures differ in relation to their architectural setting from the portal figures of French Gothic churches (FIGS. 13-15 and 13-22)? How might this be related to the changing idea of human beings in the Renaissance as opposed to the Medieval world view.

2. If you have Volume I of the text, how does Donatello's *Gattamelata* (FIG. 16-29) differ from the equestrian portrait of the emperor Marcus Aurelius (FIG. 7-59) and the Medieval *Bamberg Rider* (FIG. 13-50)? What was the apparent purpose of the high pedestal used with the *Gattemelata?*

3. Complete this question if you have Volume I of the text: Both the Church of the Katholikon (FIGS. 6-20 and 6-21) and the Pazzi Chapel (FIGS. 16-17 to 16-19) are characterized by a centralized plan, yet one is typical of Medieval Byzantine structures while the other is often used as the prime example of a Renaissance building. In what ways are the Humanism and rationality of the Renaissance apparent in Brunelleschi's building?

4. What characteristics of style are shared by Gentile da Fabriano's *Adoration of the Magi* (FIG. 16-9) and Uccello's *Battle of San Romano* (FIG. 16-22)? To what style do these characteristics relate? What feature of the Uccello work indicates that it was painted in the fifteenth century?

5. Explain the principles of linear perspective and discuss what made it so important for Renaissance artists. Select from Donatello's *Feast of Herod* (FIG. 16-3), Ghiberti's *Isaac and his Sons* (FIG. 16-5), Masaccio's *Holy Trinity* (FIG. 16-12), Uccello's *Battle of San Romano* (FIG. 16-22), Castagno's *Last Supper* (FIG. 16-37), Perigino's *Christ Delivering the Keys* (FIG. 16-40), Mantegna's *Saint James* (FIG. 16-47), and Piero's *Brera's Altarpiece* (FIG. 16-50).

6.  In what ways is Fra Angelico's *Annunciation* (FIG. 16-36) related to earlier versions like Simone Martini (FIG. 14-12)? What has he learned from artists like Masaccio?

7.  Discuss the use of space and line and the placement of the figures in Fra Filippo Lippi's *Madonna and Child with Angels* (FIG. 16-38) and Giotto's version of the same theme (FIG. 14-7). What is the religious impact of the different figure types and of the landscape background used by Fra Filippo?

8.  Compare Piero's *Finding of the True Cross* (FIG. 16-49) with *Duccio's Betrayal of Jesus* (FIG. 14-11). What chages has Piero made that lends his figures the air of monumental nobility?

9.  Discuss the way in which Alberti utilized classical  elements in the buildings he designed.

## LOOKING CAREFULLY, DESCRIBING AND ANALYZING

Write at least one page analyzing Ghirlandaio's *Birth of the Virgin* (FIG. 16-32). Here are some questions that might help you with your analysis, but do not be limited by them. Start by carefully describing the setting. What sort of a room has the artist constructed? How is the space depicted? What classical decorative elements do you see?  Then describe everything that you see within the space. How many figures are there? How do they relate to each other and how are they placed within the space? What role does each figure play in that subject? What is the subject? Is it sacred or secular? Is the setting consonant with a biblical scene? What does the setting and what do the costumes tell us about the time that the scene took place? What do you think the artist's reason was for portraying the scene as he did?

SUMMARY OF FIFTEENTH-CENTURY PAINTERS IN ITALY: EARLY RENAISSANCE

Fill in the following charts as much as possible from memory, then check your answers against the text in Chapter 16.

| Typical Examples | Stylistic Characteristics |
| --- | --- |
| Masaccio<br>City: | |
| Uccello<br>City: | |
| Gentile da Fabriano<br>City: | |
| Andrea del Castagno<br>City: | |
| Piero della Francesca<br>City: | |
| Fra Angelico<br>City: | |

Fill in the following charts as much as possible from memory, then check your answers against the text in Chapter 16.

| | Typical Examples | Stylistic Characteristics |
| --- | --- | --- |
| **Pollaiuolo**<br>City: | | |
| **Ghirlandaio**<br>City: | | |
| **Botticelli**<br>City: | | |
| **Mantegna**<br>City: | | |
| **Perugino**<br>City: | | |
| **Signorelli**<br>City: | | |

# 17

# BEAUTY, SCIENCE, AND SPIRIT IN ITALIAN ART
## THE HIGH RENAISSANCE AND MANNERISM

**TEXT PAGES  494-541**

**THE HIGH RENAISSANCE**

1.  What dates are generally accepted as the span of the High Renaissance?


2.  Name four artists who were most closely associated with the High Renaissance:

    a.                                  b.

    c.                                  d.

3.  According to Leonardo, what was the major purpose of his scientific investigations?


    What two elements did Leonardo consider to be the heart of painting?

    a.

    b.

4.  What compositional devices did Leonardo use in *The Virgin of the Rocks* (FIG. 17-1) to knit the figures together?

    a.

    b.

5.  Define the following terms and be sure you understand how their meaning related to art:

cartoon

desegno

sfumato

6.  What two fifteenth-century trends does Leonardo synthesize in *The Last Supper* (FIG. 17-3)?

a.

b

7.  Who was Julius II and why was he important for the history of art?

8.  How much of the building of the new St. Peter's was completed during Bramante's lifetime?

9.  Briefly describe four aspects of the sculptural appearance of Bramante's *Tempietto*.

a.

b.

c.

d.

10. The architect Palladio praised Bramante's *Tempietto* as the first building which had brought back "the good and beautiful architecture" of antiquity. This comment, like Michelangelo's belief that the artist must reveal the

higher truths nidden in nature comes from the Humanist revival of the
teachings of the Greek philosopher ___________________.

11. To what extent did Michelangelo utilize the mathematical procedures used
by other Renaissance sculptors to achieve harmonious proportion?

12. What is meant by the term *terribilita?*

13. List three figures that Michelangelo is believed to have created for the
tomb of Julius II.

a.                          b.                          c.

What are the two slaves thought to represent?

14. Briefly describe the iconography of the Sistine Chapel ceiling.

15. Characterize Michelangelo's style in painting and sculpture with four adjectives or
phrases.

a.

b.

c.

d.

16. What was the effect of the color revealed during the restoration of the Sistine ceiling?

17. Name the four general themes Raphael used for his paintings in the Stanza della Segnatura.

a.                                         b.


c.                                         d.

18. Who are the two central figures represented in Raphael's *School of Athens* (FIG. 17-17), and what aspects of philosophy does each represent?




19. List three characteristics of Raphael's style as seen in the *Madonna of the Meadows* (FIG. 17-19).
a.

b.

c.

20. On the death of Julius II, a son of Lorenzo de' Medici was elected as Pope

_____________, and he  became Raphael's patron.

21. The papal banker, Agostino Chigi, commissioned Raphael to decorate his villa with scenes from:


How does the central figure of the *Galatea* scene (FIG 17-20) differ from Botticelli's *Venus* (FIG. 16-27)?




22. Describe briefly the iconography of the tombs of Lorenzo and Giuliano de' Medici.

What, according to the Neo-Platonic interpretation, are the tombs thought to symbolize?

23. Who designed the Palazzo Farnese (FIGS. 17-23 and 17-24)?

How does the Farnese Palace differ from the Palazzo Medici Riccardi (FIG 16-20)?

24. What scene did Pope Paul III commission Michelangelo to paint on the altar wall of the Sistine Chapel?

25. With what urban project did Michelangelo enter the field of city planning?

What limitations did he have to cope with?

What geometric shape did he utilize to relate the various elements to one another?

26. Describe the changes Michelangelo made in Bramante's original designs for St. Peter's.

a. In the plan:

b. In the elevation:

27. What were the major formative influences on Bellini's style of painting?

28. What major  characteristics found in Bellini's *San Zaccaria Altarpiece* (FIG. 17-31) distinguishes it from the similar subject portrayed by Piero della Francesca in his *Brera Altarpiece* (FIG. 16-50)?

29. What concerns distinguish the art of Venice from that of Florence and Rome?

Venice                                  Florence and Rome

a.                                      a.

b.                                      b.

c.                                      c.

30. What does the term "poesia" mean in reference to Venetian painting?

Name a work that exemplifies this approach:

31. Briefly describe three aspects of Giorgione's style.

a.

b.

c.

32. The most outstanding feature of Titian's *Assumption of the Virgin* (FIG. 17-35) is:

33. What characteristics of Titian's *Madonna of the Pesaro Family* (FIG. 17-36) are typical of High Renaissance painting?

a.                                                      b.

What features of the work are not typical of the High Renaissance?

a.                                                    b.

34. Which of Titian's paintings established the compositional essentials for the representation of the female nude in much of later Western art?

35. Identify Isabella d'Este and explain the role she played as a patron off artists:

36. For what reason was the term "proto-baroque" applied to the work of Correggio at Parma?

**MANNERISM**

1.  Name three Mannerist painters.

a.                              b.                              c.

When did the Mannerist style emerge?

2.  List five of the characteristics of Mannerist painting that can be called "anti-Classical" and that distinguish the Mannerist from the High Renaissance style.

a.

b.

c.

d.

e.

3.  List three characteristics that Sofonisba Anguissola's *Portrait of the Artist's Sisters and Brother* (FIG. 17-46) shares with other Mannerists portraits like those by Bronzino:

a.


b.


c.

List one feature that is uniquely hers:

a.


4. Which Italian Mannerist sculptor most strongly influenced the development of French Renaissance art at Fontainebleau?



5. Which Mannerist sculptor developed the compositional device of the spiral?



6. Describe at least four features of the Palazzo del Te (FIG. 17-49) that are "irregular" from the point of view of Renaissance architectural practice.

a.


b.


c.


d.

## LATER 16th-CENTURY ARCHITECTURE

1. The mother church of the Jesuit order, whose design would be highly influential, was built in Rome between ___________ and ___________. It combined influences from a variety of sources. Identify the sources of the following:

Scroll buttresses that unite upper and lower stories:

Classical pediment:

Paired pilasters:

Plan:

**LATER 16th-CENTURY VENETIAN ART AND ARCHITECTURE**

1.  Tintoretto aspired to combine the color of ___________________ with the

    drawing of _________________.

2.  What devices does Tintoretto use to identify Christ in his version of *The Last
    Supper* (FIG. 17-52)?



    How did Leonardo identify him (FIG. 17-3)?



3.  List two characteristics of Tintoretto's painting style that point toward the
    Baroque style:

    a.

    b.

4.  Veronese's favorite subjects were

    a.                                              b.

    To what aspects of his paintings did the Holy Office of the Inquisition object?



5.  What is the difference in the type of illusion created by Veronese in *The
    Triumph of Venice* (FIG. 17-54) and that created by Correggio in *The
    Assumption of the Virgin* for the dome of Parma Cathedral (FIG. 17-41)?



6.  The state Library of San Marco in Venice (FIG. 17-55) was designed by

    _________________.

What featrure of the building seems to have been modeled after the Roman Colosseum?


What decorative scheme was used for the second story?


How did the treatment of the roofline differ from traditional practice?


In what ways does the library hamonize with the older Doge's Palace opposite it?


7.  What was most signiificant about Palladio's writings?


8.  What geometric forms did Palladio use to create the basic structure of the Villa Rotonda (FIG. 17-56)?


9.  Describe the device Palladio used for the facade of San Giorgio Maggiore (FIG. 17-58) to integrate the high central nave and low aisles.


10. In what ways does Palladio's architectural style differ from Mannerist architecture?


## DISCUSSION QUESTIONS

1.  How did the status of the visual artist change in the High Renaissance? What was the reason for this?

2.  Compare the compositions of *The Last Supper* by Leonardo (FIG. 17-3), Andrea del Casatagno (FIG. 16-37) and Dirk Bouts (FIG. 15-9) from the point of view of style, handling of space and form, and dramatic impact.

3. Why is Bramante's Tempietto often referred to as the first High Renaissance building? What are the basic qualities that distinguish it from a typical Early Renaissance building? Do you feel that the building reflects a religious attitude that is different from the Medieval one? If so, what is the difference? How is it expressed?

4. How does the iconography of the Stanza della Segnatura relate to the ideals of the High Renaissance?

5. Compare Raphael's *Galatea* (FIG. 17-20) with Botticelli's *Birth of Venus* (FIG. 16-32); note the differences in the handling of space and the representation of the bodies. What are the sources for the two subjects?

6. Compare Michelangelo's *David* (FIG. 17-9) with Polykleitos' *Doryphoros* (FIG. 5-38) and Donatello's David (FIG. 16-23) from the stylistic point of view. What similarities do you see? what differences? What distinguishes Michelangelo's *David* as a High Renaissance figure?

7. Choose a composition representative of each of the following: Raphael, Leonardo, and Michelangelo, and decide in what ways they are stylistically related and in what ways they differ. Do you think the differences relate to the personalities of the artists? Are the similarities helpful in allowing us to make any generalizations about High Renaissance style?

8. Compare Palladio's San Giorgio Maggiore (FIGS. 17-58 and 17-59) with Sant' Andrea in Mantua byAlberti (FIGS. 16-41 to 16-43). What differences do you see in the articulation of the facades and the interiors? Note also the degree of plasticity of the surfaces.

9. Compare Bronzino's *Venus, Cupid, Folly, and Time* (FIG. 17-44) with Giorgione's (and/or Titian's) *Pastoral Symphony* (FIG. 17-33). Note the poses of the figures, the settings, and the compositions. What do you think were the major concerns of each artist? How do these works reflect the different styles preferred by artists of Venice and those of Florence?

10. In what ways are the styles of the Early Renaissance in Florence, the High Renaissance in Rome, Mannerism in Florence, and the Late Renaissance in Venice typified in the portraits by Botticelli (FIG. 16-28), Raphael (FIG. 17-21), Bronzino (FIG. 17-45), and Titian (FIG. 17-39)?

11. Compare Piero's *Brera Altarpiece* (FIG. 16-50), Andrea del Sarto's *Madonnaof the Harpies* (FIG. 17-40) with Bellini's *San Zaccaria Altarpiece* (FIG. 17-31), and

Parmigianino's *Madonna with the Long Neck* (FIG. 17-43); consider the handling of space, the logic (or lack of it) of the compositions, and the treatment of the figures, including placement and proportions. What emotional effect does each artist create? Which painting do you like best? Why?

12. Compare the facade designs of Antonio da Sangallo's Farnese Palace (FIG. 17-23), Alberti's Palazzo Rucellai (FIG. 16-33)), Michelangelo's Museo Capitolino (FIG 17-27), and Giulio Romano's Palazzo del Te (FIGS. 17-49) and Sansovino's State Library (FIG. 17-55). Which building seems to be the most monumental? Why?

## LOOKING CAREFULLY AND ANALYZING

Write at least a page comparing Leonardo's *Mona Lisa* (FIG. 17-4) with Ghirlandaio's *Portrait of Giovanna Tornobouni* (FIG. 16-31). Use the terms hue, line, mass, and chiaroscuro. Here are some questions that might help you with your analysis, but do not be limited by them. What changes had Leonardo made in the pose, the handling of light and the handling of detail? Consider the placement of the figures, the definition of form, and the emotional effect achieved by each artist in creating a portrait. Which do you like better ? Why?

Fill in the following charts as much as possible from memory, then check your answers
against the text in Chapter 17.

|  | Typical Examples | Stylistic Characteristics |
|---|---|---|
| Leonardo da Vinci City: | | |
| Raphael City: | | |
| Michelangelo City: | | |
| Andrea del Sarto City: | | |
| Corregio City: | | |
| Pontormo City: | | |

SUMMARY OF SIXTEENTH-CENTURY PAINTERS IN ITALY (Continued).

|  | Typical Examples | Stylistic Characteristics |
|---|---|---|
| **Angiussola**<br>City: |  |  |
| **Parmigianino**<br>City: |  |  |
| **Bronzino**<br>City: |  |  |
| **Bellini**<br>City: |  |  |
| **Giorgioni**<br>City: |  |  |
| **Titian**<br>City: |  |  |
| **Tintoretto**<br>City: |  |  |
| **Veronese**<br>City: |  |  |

SUMMARY OF FOURTEENTH- THROUGH SIXTEENTH-CENTURY ITALIAN ART

Fill in the following charts as much as possible from memory, then check your answers against the text in Chapters 14, 16, and 17. (Note particularly pp. 423, 491 & 541)

|  | Political Leaders & Events | Cultural & Scientific Developments |
|---|---|---|
| Late Gothic |  |  |
| 15<sup>th</sup> c Florence |  |  |
| 15<sup>th</sup> c Outside Florence |  |  |
| High Renaissance |  |  |
| Mannerism |  |  |

SUMMARY OF FIFTEENTH & SIXTEENTH CENTURY ITALIAN SCULPTORS
Fill in the following charts as much as possible from memory, then check your answers against the text in Chapter 16 and 17.

|  | Typical Examples | Stylistic Characteristics |
| --- | --- | --- |
| Ghiberti<br>City: | | |
| Nanni de Banco<br>City: | | |
| Donatello<br>City: | | |
| Verrochio<br>City: | | |
| Della Robbia<br>City: | | |
| Michelangelo<br>City: | | |
| Cellini<br>City: | | |
| Giovanni da Bologna<br>City: | | |

SUMMARY OF FIFTEENTH & SIXTEENTH CENTURY ITALIAN ARCHITECTS
Fill in the following charts as much as possible from memory, then check your answers against the text in Chapter 16 and 17.

| | Typical Examples | Stylistic Characteristics |
|---|---|---|
| Brunelleschi<br>City: | | |
| Michelozzo<br>City: | | |
| Alberti<br>City: | | |
| Bramante<br>City: | | |
| Antonio da Sangallo<br>City: | | |
| Michelangelo<br>City: | | |
| Giulio Romano<br>City: | | |
| Vignola & della Porta<br>City: | | |
| Sansovino<br>City: | | |
| Palladio<br>City: | | |

# 18

# THE AGE OF THE REFORMATION
## SIXTEENTH-CENTURY ART IN NORTHERN EUROPE AND SPAIN

**TEXT PAGES 542-567**

**THE PROTESTANT REFORMATION**
1. Who was Martin Luther and what was his goal when he posted his ninety-
   five theses in Wittenburg?


2. What medium was used for  Cranach's *Allegory of Law and Grace* (FIG. 18-1)?

   Why was the medium approved by Protestants when large altarpieces were
   not?


   What image did Cranach use to describe Catholic Doctrine?


   To describe Protestant doctrine?


3. Who painted the *Isenheim Altarpiece* (FIG. 18-2 and 18-3)?


   List three characteristics of the artist's style.
   a.

   b.

   c.

63

What subject is depicted on the center panel?

On the exterior wings?

On the interior wings?

What was its purpose?

For what type of institution was the altarpiece created?

What was the reason for including Saints Sebastian and Anthony on the wings?

4.  Name the sixteenth-century Northern artist who became an international art celebrity:

5.  In what way does Dürer's representaton of the *Last Supper* (FIG. 18-4) reflect Luther's position on the sacrament of Transubstantiation?

6.  How does Dürer's support for Lutheran doctrine reflected in *The Four Apostles* (FIG. 18-5)?

7.  List two elements of Dürer's *Adam and Eve* (FIG. 18-6) that reflect his study of Italian models:

a.

b.

The poses of Adam and Eve are similar to the figures of ______________ and

_________________.

List one element that demonstrates his Northern commitment to Naturalism:

8. Name two tendencies that Dürer fuses in *Knight Death and the Devil* (FIG. 18-8)

a.

b.

9. One of Dürer's most outstanding talents was his expressive use of

_________________, whether in painting or in graphics.

10. As he began a campaign against the Turks, the Duke of Bavaria hired the

artist _____________________ to paint the historic conflict between

Alexander the Great and _____________________. In what day did the
artist emphasize the connection between the ancient battle and
contemporary times?



What stylistic effects did he utilize to emphasize the violence of the battle?



11. List three Italian elements that Holbein integrated into his painting:

a.

b.

c.

List the elements that reflect his Northern training:
a.

b.

12. What does *anamorphic* mean?


**FRANCE**
1. Who painted a famous portrait of Francis I (FIG. 18-11)?

2.  Name two Italian Mannerists who were instrumental in bringing the Mannerist style to France:

    a.                                     b.

3.  List three Manneristic characteristics that are seen in the decoration of the Gallery of Francis I at Fontainbleau (FIG. 18-12):

    a.

    b.

    c.

4.  List three Italian Renaissance  features of the Chateau of Chambord (FIG. 18-13):

    a.

    b.

    c.

    List two French Gothic features:
    a.

    b.

5.  The architect who designed the Square Court of the Louvre (FIG. 18-14) was

    ___________________ and  the sculptor who ornamented the facade was

    ___________________.

6.  Identify those features of the facade of the Louvre courtyard (FIG. 18-14) that are derived from the Italian Renaissance and those that are essentially French.

    Italian:

    a.

    b.

c.

French:

a.

b.

c.

7.  List three characteristics of Goujon's *Nymphs* from the Fountain of the Innocents (FIG. 18-15), noting which seem to be related to Italian Mannerism:

a.

b.

c.

**THE NETHERLANDS**

1.  What features of Jan Gossaert *Neptune and Amphitrite* (FIG. 18-16) are classical?



Which are not?



2.  In what ways does Quinten Massy's *Money-Changer and His Wife* (FIG. 18-17) reflect both the economic and religious life of Antwerp in the early sixteenth century? List features that relate to each.

Economic Life:


Religious life:


3.  List three religious features found in Aertsen's *Meat Still Life* (FIG. 18-18):

4. The Self-Portrait in FIG 18-19 by ________________________________ is
   purportedly the first known self-portrait by a European woman.

5. Lavina Teerlinc worked as a royal portraitist in ________________________.

6. Joachim Patiner was best known for his paintings of ________________________.

7. List three characteristics of Bruegel's landscape paintings:

   a.

   b.

   c.


**SPAIN**
1. What features of Bramante's Tempietto (FIG. 17-8) did Machuca use in the
   palace he designed for Charles V in Granada (FIG. 18-24)?




2. The Escorial was constructed for King________________________ of Spain.

   Describe the style of the building.




3. Describe two elements of El Greco's style that seem to be related to Italian
   Mannerism.
   a.

   b.

   Describe two elements that point toward the Baroque.
   a.

   b.

   Describe two purely personal stylistic traits that are found in El Greco's
   work.

a.


b.



## DISCUSSION QUESTIONS

1.  What different conceptions of the nude and of Classical mythology are apparent in Raphael's Galatea (FIG. 17-20) and Gossaert's Neptune and Amphritie (FIG. 18-16)?

2.  Compare Grunewald's *Isenheim Altarpiece* (FIGS. 18-2 and 18-3) with Jan van Eyck's *Ghent Altarpiece* (FIGS. 15-5 and 15-6). Discuss the iconography, the handling of light, color, and space, as well as the emotional impact. What kind of landscape setting does each use? How does each treat the human figure?

3.  Compare the pose and proportions of *Adam and Eve* in the representations by Van Eyck (FIG. 15-6), Massaccio (FIG. 16-11), and Durer (FIG. 18-6). How do these figures relate to classical proportions and the contrapposto pose?

4.  In what ways do you think Durer and Leonardo were alike? In what ways do you think they were different?

5.  Discuss the combination of Northern and Italinate tendencies in Durer's work, selecting from the *Last Supper* (FIG. 18-4), the *Four Apostles* (FIG. 18-5), *The Fall of Man* (FIG. 18-6), *The Great Piece of Turf* (FIG. 18-7), and *Knight Death and the Devil* (FIG. 18-8).  How might Durer's statement relate to these tendencies: "We regard a form and figure out of nature with more pleasure than any other, though the thing itself is not necessarily altogether better or worse."

6.  Compare the classicism of the Escorial (FIG. 18-8) with that of the Chateau de Chambord (FIG. 18-13). What does each building tell about the life and interests of the kings who commissioned them?

7.  What stylistic features does the work by El Greco (FIG. 18-26) share with the following artists: Parmigianino (FIG. 17-43), Tintoretto (FIG. 17-52), Cellini (FIG. 17-47), and Goujon (FIG. 18-15)? How does his work differ from theirs?

8.  Find an important Italian work that was done about the same time as
    *The Isenheim Altarpiece* (FIGS. 18-2 and 18-3) and analyze the differences
    between the works.


## LOOKING CAREFULLY, DESCRIBING AND ANALYZING

Look carefully at Holbein's *French Ambassadors* on  Fig 18-10 and write at least a
page describing and analyzing it. Here are some questions that might help you with
your analysis, but do not be limited by them. First look at the space that is defined in
the composiition. Examine the floor, the curtain and the table. What is on the table?
See how many objects you can find and then carefully describe each of them,
considering the texture, the pattern and the color of each, and whether or not
foreshortening was used. What do you think each object was used for? Describe the
strange object in the lower center of the picture. What is it, and how did Holbein
depict it? What relation might it have to the two men?

Next describe the two figures : the clothes they wear; the way they stand.
How does Holbein indicate their position in space? Does one seem more
dominant than the other? What do the objects on the table tell us about each
of them? Which do you think belonged to each man? What do you think
each of the men did for a living, based on what Holbein shows us? What do
the expressions on their faces tell us about their personalities. Which one do
you think you would like the most? Why?

# MAP

Circle the following on the map below.

Nuremberg     Basel     Granada     Toledo     Antwerp     Madrid

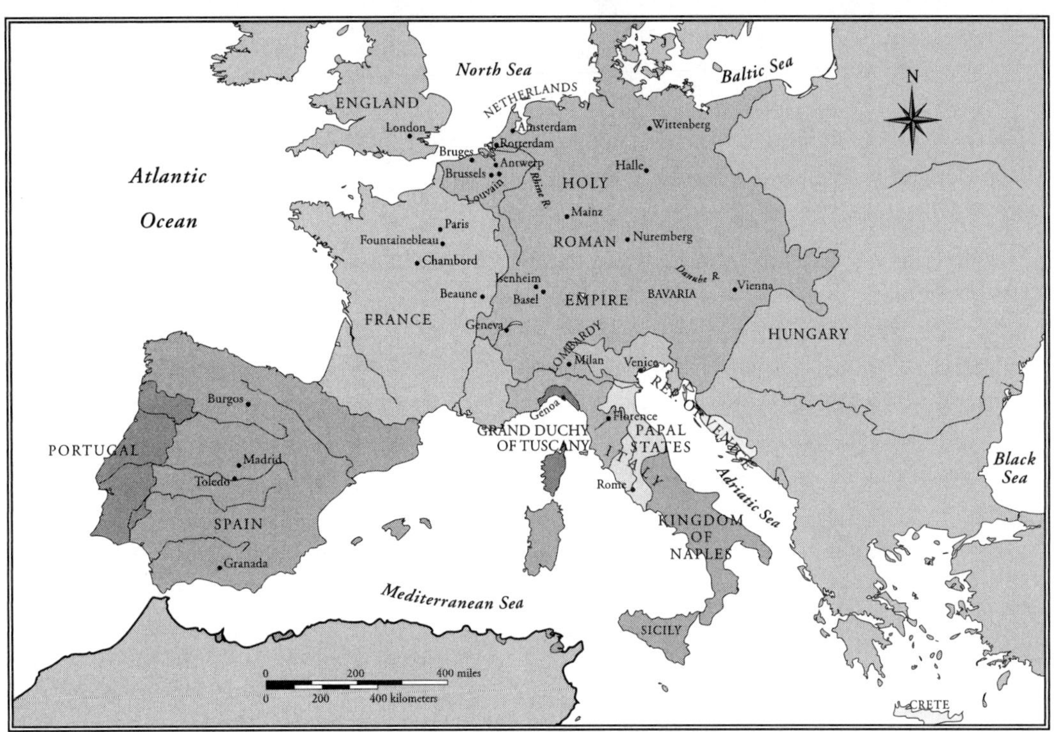


**MAP 18-1** Europe in the 16th Century

# SUMMARY OF FOURTEENTH THROUGH SIXTEENTH CENTURY ART IN NORTHERN EUROPE AND SPAIN

Fill in the following charts as much as possible from memory, then check your answers against the text in Chapters 15 and 18. (Note particularly pp. 451 & 567)

|  | Political Leaders & Events | Cultural & Scientific Developments |
|---|---|---|
| 15$^{th}$ c Netherlands |  |  |
| 16$^{th}$ c Netherlands |  |  |
| 15$^{th}$ c France |  |  |
| 15$^{th}$ c Germany |  |  |
| 16$^{th}$ c Germany |  |  |

## SUMMARY OF SIXTEENTH-CENTURY PAINTERS IN THE NETHERLANDS

Fill in the following charts as much as possible from memory, then check your answers against the text in Chapter 18.

|  | Typical Examples | Stylistic Characteristics |
|---|---|---|
| Massys |  |  |
| Gossaert |  |  |
| Aertsen |  |  |
| van Hemessen |  |  |
| Teerling |  |  |
| Bruegel |  |  |
| Patiner |  |  |

## SUMMARY OF FRENCH RENAISSANCE ART

Fill in the following charts as much as possible from memory, then check your answers against the text in Chapter 18.

| Typical Examples |  | Stylistic Characteristics |
|---|---|---|
| Clouet |  |  |
| Rosso Fiorentino at Fontainbleu |  |  |
| Goujon |  |  |
| Lescot |  |  |

SUMMARY OF GERMAN RENAISSANCE ART
Fill in the following charts as much as possible from memory, then check your answers
against the text in Chapter 18.

Typical Examples    Stylistic Characteristics

Lochner


Witz


Stoss


Wolgemut

Schongauer


Altdorfer


Cranach


Gruenewald


Durer


Holbein

# 19

# POPES, PEASANTS, MONARCHS AND MERCHANTS
## BAROQUE ART

**TEXT PAGES 568-627**

**BAROQUE ART IN THE 17TH CENTURY**
1.  With what religious movement is much of the Baroque art in Catholic countries associated?

    List three adjectives or phrases that describe its style:

    a.

    b.

    c.

2.  What city was the focus of artistic patronage as the  Catholic church tried to reestablish its primacy?

3.  List three ways in which Madern's Early Baroque church of Santa Susanna (FIG. 19-1) resembles the church of Il Gesu (FIG. 17-49):

    a.

    b.

    c.

List three ways in which it differs:

a.


b.


c.


4. Name four architects who worked on St. Peter's and note the primary
   contribution of each.

a.

b.

c.

d.

5. What is a *baldacchino?*


6. List four major characteristics of Bernini's sculpture that are typical of
   Baroque art in general.

a.

b.

c.

d.

7. In what way did Bernini depict the vision of St. Theresa  (FIG 19-9)?

8. Who developed the "sculptural" architectural style to its extreme?

Name two buildings designed by him.

a.                                              b.

Both are located in the city of ________________________.

9. While the circle had been the ideal geometric figure to Renaissance
architects,

Baroque planners preferred the ________________________.

Why?

10. What is the purpose of the lateral, three-part division of Baroque palace
facades?

Upon what human psychological tendency does it seem to be based?

11. Name two countries were the architectural styles of Borromini and Guarini
particularly influential?

a.                                              b.

12. The common purpose of Caravaggio's *Conversion of St. Paul* (FIG. 19-18) and
Bernini's *The Ecstasy of St. Theresa* (FIG. 19-9) was:

13. List three characteristics of Caravaggio's style.

a.

b.

c.

14. What was Caravaggio attempting to present in his religious pictures?


What pictorial devices did he use to achieve his goal?



15. What is *tenebroso*?


List two countries where it was particularly inflential:

a.                                        b.

16. Which artists most influenced the style of Artemesia Gentileschi?

Who were Judith and Holophernes?

What techniques does Artemesia use to portray the drama of the theme?


17. List three assumptions that were basic to the teaching of art at the Bolognese
academy.

a.

b.

c.

18. Who is credited with developing the "classical" or "ideal" landscape?


What were its roots?


19. What earlier work strongly influenced Annibale Carracci's ceiling frescoes in
the gallery of the Farnese Palace in Rome (FIG. 19-23)?

How did Carracci modify the original to achieve heightened illusionism?


20. What is *quadro riportato* and how was it used?


21. Name two influences blended by Reni in his Aurora fresco (FIG. 19-24):

a.

b.

22. List three ways in which Pietro da Cortona's frescoed ceiling in the Palazzo
Barberini (FIG. 19-25) praised his patron:

a.

b.

c.

23. What effect did Gaulli create with the fresco he painted on the ceiling of Il Gesu
in Rome (FIG. 19-26):

List three devices he used to achieve that effect:

a.

b.

c.

24. The panter beside Gaulli who worked for the Jesuits in Rome was

__________________. He painted  the ceiling of the church of

__________________ for them.

What device did he use to merge  heaven and earth?

25. Name two Spanish rulers from the Hapsburg dynasty who were patrons of the arts:

a.                                              b.

26. What  was the goal of many Spanish Baroque religious artists?


Name a theme that was particularly popular among them:


27. Ribera's style was influenced by the "dark manner" of:


28. What type of lighting did Zurbaran  use in his pating of *Saint Serapion* (FIG. 19-29)?


29. Velazquez was court painter to King _____________________________.

30. What does Velasquez's *Surrender of Breda* (FIG. 19-31) commemorate?


31. What is the subject of *Las Meninas* (FIG. 19-33)?

How many levels of reality can you find in the picture?

Briefly describe them.


What painting technique did Velazquez use in *Las Meninas?*


32. The northern provinces constitute the modern country of _____________________________,

while those in the south constitute the country of _____________________________.

During the seventeenth century, this southern region was known as _____________________.

33. In his *Elevation of the Cross* (FIG. 19-34) Rubens  synthesized his study of classical

antiquity with the work of the Italian masters_________________,

_________________and_________________ while adding his own dynamism.

List three features that contribute to the drama of the scene:

a.

b.

c.

34. What member of the famous Florentine House of Medici commissioned
Rubens to paint a cycle memorializing and glorifying her career and that of
her late husband?


35. Name the painting that embodies Rubens' attitude toward war:

What did the followng allegorical figures symbolize?

Monsters:

Woman with a broken lute:

Architect fallen backwards:

Book and paper at the feet of Mars:

Sorrowing woman in black:


36. In what type of paintings did Van Dyck specialize?

How could his style best be characterized?

37. In what type of subject matter did Clara Peeters specialize?


38. How did the religious and economic conditions in seventeenth-century
    Holland effect artistic  patronage and production?

    a.

    b.

    c.

39. In what way was the work of Gerrit van Honthorst influenced by
    Caravaggio?


40. Frans Hals was the leading painter of the_______________________school,

    and specialized  in_______________________________.

    What are the main elements of his style that distinguish his works from
    those of his contemporaries?


    Write down two adjectives that describe his style:

    a.                                              b.

41. Who commissioned Rembrandt to paint *The Anatomy of Dr. Tulp* (FIG. 19-
    44)?


    What does this tell us about paronage in Holland during the 17th century?


42. What feature of *The Company of Captain Frans Fanning Coq* (FIG. 19-45) led to
    its being misnamed *The Night Watch*?


    What devices did Rembrant use to enliven the group portrait?

43. List three adjectives or phrases  that would contrast Rembrandt's religious
works to Counter-Reformation art works:

a.

b.

c.

44. What was Rembrandt trying to express in his portraits and self-portraits?

45. Briefly describe Rembrandt's use of light and shade.

How does his use of light and shade effect the mood of his later portraits?

46. Briefly describe the technique of etching.

What are its advantages over engraving?

47. For what genre was the Dutch painter Judith Leyster most famous?

What characteristic did she share with Hals?

48. What  reason could be given for the Dutch interest in landscape painting?

Name two artists who specialized in it:

a.                                                              b.

49. What was Vermeer's favorite type of subject matter?

50. In what way does Vermeer's use of light differ from Rembrandt's?

51. On what principle does a *camera obscura* work?

52. List three important facts about the optics of color that are illustrated in Vermeer's paintings:

a.

b.

c.

53. How does  the mood created by Steen's interiors differ from that created by Vermeer's?

54. What might the children's behavior symbolize in Steen's *Feast of St. Nicholas* (FIG. 19-54)?

55. What is a "Vanitas" still life?

56. The paintings of Rachael Ruysch reflect a particular interest in:

57. Which French artist is credited with having established seventeenth-century Classical painting?

Where did he spend most of his life?

What two Italian artists did he most admire?

58. What four characteristics of *Et in Arcadia Ego*(FIG. 19-58) are typical of Poussin's fully developed Classical style?

a.

b.

c.

d.

59. What type of subjects did Poussin consider to be appropriate for paintings done in the "grand manner"?

What did he think should be avoided?

60. Poussin and Rubens were considered as the two poles in the Baroque debate between the forces of passion and reason. Which pole do you think each artist represented? What characteristics in the work of each artist do you thinnk would reflect those attitudes?

Rubens:

Poussin:

61. In what major way does the landscape in Poussin's *Burial of Phocion* (FIG. 19-59) differ from Van Ruisdael's *View of Haarlem* (FIG. 19-51)?

62. What was Claude Lorrain's primary interest in landscape painting?

In what country did he do most of his painting?

63. Describe the features that create the impression of dignity and sobriety
apparent in Mansart's work at Blois (FIG. 19-61).

a.

b.

What feature of the building is typically Baroque?

64. The life of French peasants was the favorite subject of
_______________________.

How do his depictions differ from those of the Dutch painter Jan Steen?

65. The French artist Callot is best known for his works done in the medium of

_______________.

His *Miseries* series realistically depicts scenes of
_______________________________.

66. Which French artist was most influenced by the northern "Caravaggisti"?

In what ways does his style differ from theirs?

67. The French Royal Academy of Painting and Sculpture was established in the

year _________.

What was its primary purpose?

68. What was the political meaning of Louis XIV's appelation "le Roi Soleil" (the
Sun King)?

What was his significance as a patron of the arts?

69. List three features of Rigaud's Portrait of Louis XIV (FIG. 19-65) that contributed to Louis' personification of an absolute monarch:

a.

b.

c.

70. What three architects collaborated to design the east facade of the Louvre?

a.                          b.                          c.

What form was used for the central pavilion of the facade?

71. Who was the principal director for the building and decoration of the Palace of Versailles?

Who designed the park of Versailles?

What was symbolized by the vast complex of Versailles?

72. List two sources for Girardon's portrayal of Apollo Attended by the Nymphs carved for the Park of Versailles (FIG. 19-70):

a.                          b.

73. Which feature of Jules Hardouin-Mansart's Church of the Invalides (FIG. 19-72) is most Baroque?

Which is most classical?

74. Which of the visual or plastic arts was most important in seventeenth-century England?

75. Name the Italian architect who had the strongest influence on the buildings of Inigo Jones?

76. Who designed St. Paul's Cathedral in London?

What feature of the building shows the influence of Borromini?

What feature is taken over from the east facade of the Louvre?

## LATE BAROQUE ART OF THE EARLY EIGHTEENTH CENTURY
1.  Blenheim Palace in England (FIG. 19-75) was designed by

_______________________for_____________________.

However, before it was completed it was criticized as being

__________________.

2.  Who designed the church of Vierzehnheiligen (FIG. 19-76, 19-77)?

3.  Theatrical illuisionism is an important characteristic of the work of the

German Baroque sculptor: _____________________.

4.  Which eighteenth-century Italian painter is best known for his elegant illusionistic ceiling paintings?

# DISCUSSION QUESTIONS

1. Study the elevations and plans of Bramanti's Pazzi Chapel (FIGS. 16-17 to 16-19) and Borromini's San Carlo alle Quattro Fontane (FIGS. 19-10 and 19-11). Contrast the basic shapes used in the plans, and describe how these forms relate to the elevations of the buildings.

2. Bernini's art has been described as "theatrical." Give examples of its theatricality and discuss the technical devices he used to create them.

3. Compare Ribera's *Martyrdom of St. Bartholomew* (FIG. 19-28) with Mantegna's *St. James Led to Martyrdom* (FIG. 16-47). Discuss composition, painting technique, and emotional impact. What major concerns of the Italian Renaissance and the Counter-Reformation in Spain are demonstrated by these works?

4. Discuss the influence of Caravaggio on Gerrit van Honthorst (FIG. 19-41), George de la Tour (FIG. 19-64), and Louis le Nain (FIG. 19-62). Which aspects of Caravaggio's style did each adopt, and how do their works differ from him and from each other?

5. In what ways do the works and lives of Rubens and Rembrandt reflect the different social and religious orientations of seventeenth-century Flanders and Holland?

6. Compare Rembrandt's *Self-Portrait* (FIG. 19-47) with the self-portraits by Judith Leyster (FIG. 19-49) and  Caterina van Hemessen (FIG. 18-19), and Van Eyck's *Man in a Red Turban* (FIG 15-10) How have the artists depicted the different psychological states as they look at themselves? Do you think these works illustrate major differences in the philosophies of the times and/or places where painted or that the interpretations were solely indivisual? Why?

7. What was the effect of the economic and religious climate of seventeenth-century Holland on its artists?

8. Discuss the relative balance between Baroque and Renaissance features in the following buildings: the east facade of the Louvre (FIG. 19-66), the Church of the Invalides in Paris (FIG. 19-72), the Banqueting House at Whitehall (FIG. 19-73), and St. Paul's Cathedral in London (FIG. 19-74).

9. In what ways did Louis XIV influence French art of the seventeenth century? How did his utilization of art differ from that of Philip IV in Spain?

10. Could Velásquez's *Surrender at Breda* (FIG. 19-31) and Steen's *Feast of St. Nicholas* (FIG. 19-54) serve as illustrations of Poussin's "grand manner"? If not, why not?

11. Who was chiefly responsible for the development of "classical" landscape painting in Italy? How did his approach differ from those of Poussin (FIG. 19-58), Claude Lorrain (FIG. 19-60), and Van Ruisdael (FIG. 19-51)?

12. Compare the ceiling paintings of Tiepolo (FIG. 19-79) with those of Mantegna (FIG, 17-46), Veronese (FIG, 16-54), Correggio (FIG, 17-41), Caracci (FIG, 19-23), Pietro da Cortona (FIG, 19-25), and Pozzo (FIG, 19-27). Which is closest to his work, and what features do they share?

13. From the other works you have studied, which do you feel are closest in spirit to Neumann's pilgrimage church of Vierzehnheiligen (FIGS, 19-76 and 24-77) and Asam's *Assumption of the Virgin* (FIG. 19-78)?

## LOOKING CAREFULLY, DESCRIBING AND ANALYZING

In *Las Meninas* Velásquez demonstrated his mastery of the depiction of complex levels of visual reality(p.568 and FIG. 19-33). Study the painting very carefully and write an essay of at least one page describing it. Here are some questions that might help you with your analysis, but do not be limited by them. First describe the room in which he has placed the majority of the figures and describe each of the figures in that space. Then look for other figures an describe the space in which they would be standing. Describe the artist's brushwork and his use of light and dark and note he uses these elements to increase the sense of reality of the scene.

# MAP

Circle the following on the map below.

Haarlem       Utrecht       Amsterdam       Versailles       London

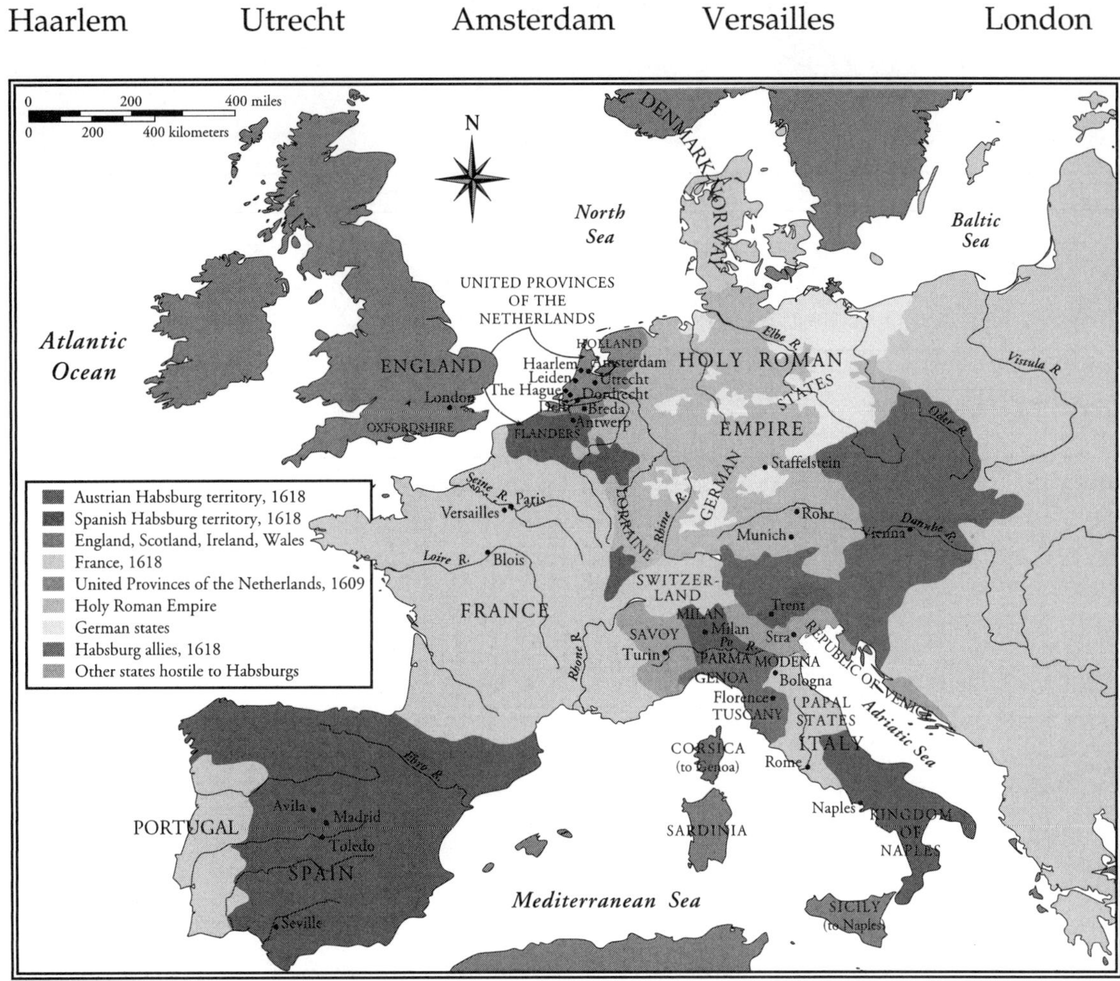


**MAP 19-1** Europe at the onset of the Thirty Years' War

SUMMARY OF EIGHTEENTH-CENTURY PAINTING & SCULPTURE

Fill in the following charts as much as possible from memory, then check your answers against the text in Chapter 19. (Note particularly p. 627)

BACKGROUND:     Historical People, Events, Ideas, etc

| PAINTING: | Typical Examples | Stylistic Characteristics |
| --- | --- | --- |
| Tiepolo (see ch. 17)<br>Country: | | |
| Watteau<br>Country: | | |
| Boucher<br>Country: | | |
| Fragonard<br>Country: | | |
| Greuze<br>Country: | | |
| Wright of Derby<br>Country: | | |
| Chardin<br>Country: | | |
| Vigee-Lebrun<br>Country: | | |
| Hogarth<br>Country: | | |
| Gainsborough<br>Country: | | |

## SUMMARY OF EIGHTEENTH-CENTURY PAINTING & SCULPTURE (Continued)

Typical Examples        Stylistic Characteristics

West
Country:

Copley
Country:

Canaletto
Country:

Kauffman
Country:

David
Country:

Piranesi
Country:

Fuseli
Country:

Blake
Country:

Clodion
Country:

Canova
Country:

Lewis
Country:

SUMMARY OF EIGHTEENTH-CENTURY ARCHITECTS
Fill in the following charts as much as possible from memory, then check your answers
against the text in Chapter 19.

| | Typical Examples | Stylistic Characteristics |
|---|---|---|
| Boffrand<br>Country: | | |
| Cuvilliers<br>Country: | | |
| Derby &<br>Prichard<br>Country: | | |
| Boyle &<br>Kent<br>Country: | | |
| Wood<br>Country: | | |
| Adam<br>Country: | | |
| Jefferson<br>Country: | | |
| Latrobe<br>Country: | | |
| Soufflot<br>Country: | | |

SUMMARY OF BAROQUE ART

Fill in the following charts as much as possible from memory, then check your answers against the text in Chapter 19. (Note particularly p. 627)

|  | Political Leaders & Events | Cultural & Scientific Developments |
| --- | --- | --- |
| ITALY:<br>Religious<br>Orientation? |  |  |
| SPAIN:<br>Religious<br>Orientation? |  |  |
| FLANDERS:<br>Religious<br>Orientation? |  |  |
| HOLLAND:<br>Religious<br>Orientation: |  |  |
| FRANCE:<br>Religious<br>Orientation? |  |  |
| ENGLAND:<br>Religious<br>Orientation? |  |  |
| GERMANY:<br>Religious<br>Orientation? |  |  |

SUMMARY OF BAROQUE PAINTING AND SCULPTURE
Fill in the following charts as much as possible from memory, then check your answers
against the text in Chapter 19.

| | Typical Examples | Stylistic Characteristics |
| --- | --- | --- |
| Annibale Carracci<br>Country: | | |
| Reni<br>Country: | | |
| Caravaggio<br>Country: | | |
| Gaulli<br>Country: | | |
| Gentilschi<br>Country: | | |
| Pozzo<br>Country: | | |
| Ribera<br>Country: | | |
| Zurbaran<br>Country: | | |
| Velazquez<br>Country: | | |

| Typical Examples | Stylistic Characteristics |
| --- | --- |
| **Rubens**<br>Country: | |
| **van Dyck**<br>Country: | |
| **Peters**<br>Country: | |
| **Honthorst**<br>Country: | |
| **Terbruggen**<br>Country: | |
| **Hals**<br>Country: | |
| **Rembrandt**<br>Country: | |
| **Vermeer**<br>Country: | |
| **Leyster**<br>Country: | |

| Typical Examples | Stylistic Characteristics |
| --- | --- |
| Ruysch<br>Country: | |
| van Ruisdael<br>Country: | |
| Rigaud<br>Country: | |
| De la Tour<br>Country: | |
| Le Nain<br>Country: | |
| Poussin<br>Country: | |
| Claude Lorrain<br>Country: | |
| Tiepolo<br>Country: | |
| Bernini<br>Country: | |
| Girardon<br>Country: | |
| Assam<br>Country: | |

## SUMMARY OF BAROQUE ARCHITECTS

Fill in the following charts as much as possible from memory, then check your answers against the text in Chapter 19.

| | Typical Examples | Stylistic Characteristics |
|---|---|---|
| **Maderno**<br>Country: | | |
| **Bernini**<br>City: | | |
| **Boromini**<br>City: | | |
| **Guarini**<br>Country: | | |
| *Louvre*<br>City:<br>Architects: | | |
| *Versailles*<br>Country:<br>Architects: | | |
| **Hardouin-Mansart**<br>Country: | | |
| **Vanbrugh**<br>Country: | | |
| **Neuman**<br>Country: | | |

# ICONOGRAPHIC SUMMARY

While stylistic analysis tells us how a thing is represented, iconographic analysis helps us understand what is represented.  Images of saints, biblical, and mythological figures are usually identified by certain attributes that are associated with their particular story.  Look at the representations of the following religious figures is Chapters 14 through 19 and briefly describe the way you would identify them in terms of their iconography:

| |
|---|
| St. Anthony |
| St. Catherine |
| David |
| St. Francis |
| St. George |
| Judith (with Holofernes) |
| Mary Magdalene |
| Moses |
| St. John the Baptist |
| St. Peter |
| St. Paul |
| St. James |
| St. Stephen |
| St. Theresa |

# 20

# THE ENLIGHENMENT AND ITS LEGACY
## ART OF THE LATE 18TH THROUGH THE MID 19TH CENTURY

**TEXT PAGES  628-683**

**ROCOCO: THE FRENCH TASTE**

1. List four adjectives that describe the type of art created for the eighteenth-century French aristocracy:

   a.                                       b.


   c.                                       d.


2. Compare the photographs of the Salon de la Princess of the Hotel de Soubise (FIG 20-1) and the Galerie des Glaces de Versailles (FIG. 19-69). List three adjectives or phrases that describe each:

   Salon de la Princess                     Galerie des Glaces
   a.                                       a.

   b.                                       b.

   c.                                       c.

   d.                                       d.


3. One of the best examples of French Rococo architecture, known as the

   _______________ was built near  Munich, Germany. It was designed by

   __________.

   List three Rococo features of this small building:

   a.

b.

c.


4.  What is a fête galant?


5.  What two seventeenth-century artists inspired the debate in eighteenth-century France between the advantages of color as the most important element in painting and those of form?

Color:                                   Form:

Which element did Watteau consider to be the most important?


6.  List four characteristics of Watteau's *Return from Cythera* (FIG. 20-4) that are typical of Rococo art in general:

a.

b.

c.

d.


7.  List three Baroque devices used by Boucher in *Cupid a Captive* (FIG. 20-5):

a.

b.

c.


8.  In what way does Fragonard's *The Swing* (FIG. 20-6) typify a Rococo "intrigue" picture?

9.  Name a sculptor who worked in The Rococo style:

List three characteristics of his work:

a.

b.

c.


**THE ENLIGHTENMENT: PHILOSOPHY AND SOCIETY/ SCIENCE AND TECHNOLOGY**

1. What is meant by the "Age of Enlightenment," and how did it affect the role of art?


2. List two ways in which European art was changed as a result of the scientific and technological advances made from the end of the eighteenth through the early nineteenth centuries?

a.

b.


3. In what ways does Wright of Derby's *Philosopher Giving a Lecture at the Orrery* (FIG. 20-9) reflect the scientific view of the universe?


Would this painting be considered as an appropriate subject for Poussin's "Grand Manner"?

Why or why not?


4. Describe the type of lighting that was often used by Joseph Wright of Derby:

5.  What was the significance of the Coalbrookdale bridge (FIG. 20-10)?

**VOLTAIRE VERSUS ROUSSEAU: SCIENCE VERSUS THE TASTE FOR THE "NATURAL"**

1.  Who was Voltaire?

2.  What, according to Rousseau, had corrupted the "natural man"?

    How did his views differ from those of Voltaire?

3.  What effect did Rousseau's views have on eighteenth-century French art?

4.  Sentimentality and moralizing are obvious traits of the work of the French

    painter _________________.

5.  From what social class did the majority of Chardin's patrons come?

    Why did his work appeal to them?

6.  The French painter Elisabeth Louise Vigée-Lebrun specialized
    in___________.

    In contrast to Rococo artificiality, the style of her self-portrait (FIG. 20-13) can
    be described as:

7.  What type of subject matter did Hogarth portray?

8. Although Gainsborough preferred to paint landscapes, he is best known for

his _____________________. Briefly describe his style:

   To what genre did Gainsborough's portraits belong?

 9. For what type of portraits is Sir Joshua Reynolds most famous?

10. Name an American painter who was influential in the Anglo-American
    school of history painting:

11. How does Copley's portrait of *Paul Revere* (FIG. 20-18) differ from
    contemporary British and continental portraits?

12. What is a *veduta* painting?

**THE REVIVAL OF INTEREST IN CLASSICISM**
1.  Neoclassicism was stimulated by the excavation of the Roman cities of

_______________and _________________ in the mid _______________.

2.  Angelica Kauffmann combined two styles in her work. What were they?

   a.                                          b.

3.  What is the importance of the subject matter in the *Oath of the Horatii* (FIG. 20-
    21)?

List two Neoclassical stylistic features that are found in that work:

a.

b.


4.  Briefly explain the politics behind David's *Death of Marat* (FIG. 20-22):




5.  For what major patron did David work after the fall of the Revolutionary party?


6.  In what ways does the *Coronation of Napoleon* (FIG 20-23) document the relationship between church and state?



    What Neoclassic features are apparent in the painting?


7.  What provided the inspiration for Soufflot's design for the church of Ste. Genevieve (now the Pantheon) in Paris (FIG. 20-24)?


8.  What was the original purpose of La Madeleine (FIG. 20-25)?

    What are its primary stylistic features?


9.  Which aspect of Canova's portrait of Pauline Borghese (FIG. 20-26) comes from the earlier Rococo style?

    Which aspect is realistic?

Which features are Neoclassical?

10. In reaction to Baroque buildings like Blenheim, the restraint of

    _______________ was restated in buildings like Chiswick House (FIG. 20-27).

    Chiswick House was designed by _______________ and _______________.

    List four of its stylistic features:

    a.

    b.

    c.

    d.

11. What is important about the Royal Crescent at Bath (FIG. 20-28)?

12. What was the significance of the work of Robert Adam?

13. Name two buildings that apparently influenced Jefferson's designs for
    Monticello:

    a.                                      b.

14. Why did Jefferson believe that the Neoclasssic style was appropriate for the
    architecture of the new American republic?

15. What is the name of the sculptor who carved *Forever Free* (FIG. 20-33)?

    What is its political significance?

16. Name three of David's pupils:

a.                          b.                          c.

17. In what respect does Gros' *Pest House at Jaffa* (FIG. 20-34) differ stylistically
from David's *Oath of the Horatii* (FIG. 20-21)?

18. What is the supposed setting for Girodet-Troison's *Burial of Atala* (FIG. 20-35)?

What story does it tell?

19. In breaking with David, Ingres adopted a manner that he felt was based on
true and pure Greek style. List two characteristics of that style:

a.                                         b.

20. What did Ingres use as the model for the composition of his *Apotheosis of
Homer* (FIG. 20-36)?

21. Name two Renaissance artists whose influence is apparent in Ingres' *Grande
Odalisque* (FIG. 20-37):
a.                                         b.

22. Scholars use the term "Romanticism to refer to a general phenomenon that

began around _________ and ended around ________. It can also be used more

narrowly as the name of a movement that flourished between _________ and

_________.

23. The shift from reason to feeling, from objective nature to subjective emotion,
is characteristic of the attitude of mind known as:

List three values that were stressed during the so-called Age of Sensibility:

a.

b.

c.

24. What feelings were thought to be evoked by the "sublime" in nature and art?



25. How does Piranesi's Carceri 14 (FIG. 20-38) illustrate eighteenth-century taste for the sublime?



26. What type of subject matter was typically found in the work of Henry Fuseli?



27. Who was William Blake?


Briefly characterize his style:



28. Goya's work cannot be confined to a single stylistic classification.  Briefly summarize his varied concerns as expressed in the following works:

*Sleep of Reason Produces Monsters* (FIG. 20-41):


*The Family of Charles IV* (FIG. 20-42):


*The Third of May, 1808* (FIG. 20-43):

*Saturn Devouring his Children* (FIG. 20-44):

29. What was the political message behind Gericault's *Raft of the Medusa* (FIG. 20-45)?

   List three devices he used to add drama to his presentation:

   a.

   b.

   c.

30. The portrait shown on FIG. 20-46 illustrates Gericault's interest in

   _______________.

31. The seventeenth-century debate between the Poussinists and the Rubenists

   was carried on in the nineteenth century by _______________, the

   draftsman, and _______________, the colorist.

32. List four characteristics of Delacroix's style that are seen in *The Death of Sardanapalus* (FIG. 20-47):

   a.

   b.

   c.

   d.

   What does the scene depict and how does the subject relate to the interests of the Romantics?

33. What political event did Delacroix depict in *Liberty Leading the People* (FIG. 20-48)?

34. List three romantic interests embodied in *The Tiger Hunt* (FIG. 20-49):

   a.

   b.

   c.

35. Write down one of Delacroix's observations on the way to apply color to the canvas:

36. What did Rude portray in *La Marseillaise* (FIG. 20-50)?

   What similarities do you see to Delacroix's *Liberty Leading the People* (FIG. 20-48)?

   What differences?

37. List three Romantic concerns that you see in Bayre's *Jaguar Devouring a Hare* (FIG. 20-51):

   a.

   b.

   c.

**IMAGINATION AND MOOD IN LANDSCAPE PAINTING**
1.  What did Caspar David Friedrich believe that the artist should paint?

2.  What sorts of scenes did Constable like to paint?

How did he create the sparkling effect of light?

In what way could his work be related to the Romantic outlook?

3.  How does Turner's *Slave Ship* (FIG. 20-54) reflect the practices of nineteenth-century slave traders?

List three adjectives that describe Turner's style:

a.                              b.                              c.

What features of Turner's work were most influential in liberating artists from the traditional way of painting?

4.  To what school of art did Thomas Cole belong?

5.  Name two artists who painted views of the landscape of the western United States:

a.                                        b.

What relationship did their paintings have to the doctrine of Manifest Destiny?

## VARIOUS REVIVALIST STYLES IN ARCHITECTURE

1.  What style did Barry and Pugin use for the rebuilding of the Houses of Parliament in London (FIG. 20-58)?

2.  What relationship does the style of Nash's Royal Pavilion in Brighton (FIG. 20-59) have to British Imperialism?

3.  List three features that the Paris Opera House (FIG. 20-60) shares with the east façade of the Louvre (FIG. 19-66):

a.

b.

c.

4..  Describe the effect of the use of iron on nineteenth-century architectural structures:

5.  What was the significance of the techniques used by Paxton to construct the Crystal Palace (FIG. 20-62)?

6.  Who was Eugene Durieu, and why is he important for the history of painting?

7.  What is the difference between the *camera obscura* and the *camera lucida*?

8.  When did Daguerre present his new photographic process in Paris?

Briefly describe the Daguerrotype process:

In general, how did artists react to Daguerre's invention?

9.  What is a calotype?


Who developed it and when?


10. For what type of work were Nadar and Cameron most famous?


11. Name two photographers who documented the American civil War:

a.                                              b.


## DISCUSSION QUESTIONS

1.  Compare Fragonard's *The Swing* (FIG. 20-6) with Bronzino's *Cupid, Folly and Time* (FIG 17-24). Although both works have strong erotic overtones, they are very different in their emotional effects. What makes one Rococo and the other Mannerist?

2.  In what way does Rousseau's statement "Man is born free, but everywhere in chains" reflect the premises of romanticism? Select three images that you think illustrate this view and explain why they do.

3.  Discuss the influence of Palladian classicism on eighteenth-century architecture.

4.  Compare Benjamin West's *Death of General Wolfe* (FIG. 20-17) with el Greco's *Burial of Count of Orgaz* (FIG. 18-26). Note stylistic similarities and differences and explain the iconographic features that make one a Baroque painting and the other a product of the Enlightenment.

5.  Compare Ingres' *Grande Odalisque* (FIG. 20-37) with Titian's *Venus of Urbino* (FIG. 17-38) How do they differ in composition, body type, distortion, and degree of idealization?

6.  Do you think there are remnants of Romanticism alive today in our society? If so, can you identify them? How are they reflected in the arts? What film

that you have seen recently best embodies the ideas of romanticism?  Can you
think of an artist working today that you would consider to be a Romantic?

7.  Discuss the differences in approach to the depiction of landscape in the works
    of Poussin (FIG. 19-59 ),  Ruisdale (FIG. 19-51), Canaletto (FIG. 20-19), Turner
    (FIG. 20-54), Constable (FIG. 20-53),  Cole (FIG. 20-55), Bierstadt (FIG. 20-56),
    Church (FIG. 20-57), and Friedrich (FIG. 20-52).

8.  Compare Watteau's *Return from Cythera* (FIG. 20-4) with Wright of Derby's *A
    Lecture at the Orrery* (FIG. 20-9), Hogarth's *Breakfast Scene from Marriage a la
    Mode* (FIG. 20-14), Goya's *The Third of May, 1808* (FIG. 20-43), David's *Oath of
    the Horatii* (FIG. 20-21), and Delacroix's *Liberty Leading the People* (FIG. 20-54).
    What is the style and the social message of each? Which do you feel is most
    effective with getting that message across? Why?


### DESCRIBING, ANALYZING AND RELATING TO A SOCIAL MESSAGE

Look carefully at Hogarth's *Breakfast Scene* from *Marriage `a la Mode* (FIG. 20-14) and
David's *Oath of the Horatii* (FIG. 20-21). Both images contain social commentary, yet
their messages and their styles are quite different. Write at least two pages analyzing
and comparing them. Here are some questions that might help you with your
analysis, but do not be limited by them.

First look at the spaces and the figures within them. Describe the architectural
setting and any accessories you see. Then look at the figures.  How many figures are
there, and how do they relate to each other and to the spaces the artist has created?
What are the figures wearing and how do the costumes relate to the message the
artist is trying to convey? What historical period is each depicting? Look at the poses
of the individual figures; what does the pose of each figure tell us about the
personality and motivation of that figure?

What was the political background in which each image was created? What style did
each artist use and how might the style have been important is the artist's message?
Why might one of the artists have used a classical theme while the other created a
stage set? What was the social purpose of each image ; what was each artist trying to
get people to do or think? How effective do you think each artist was?

# 21

# THE RISE OF MODERNISM
## ART OF THE LATER 19TH CENTURY

**TEXT PAGES  684-733**

**THE DEVELOPMENT OF MODERNISM**

1. List three nineteenth-century phenomena that the authors believe contributed to the greaterconsciouness of modernity, "the state of being modern."

    a.

    b.

    c.

    What effect did this "Modernist" consciousness  have on artists?


2. Although hailed as the father of Realism, Courbet did not like to be called a Realist. What can we gather from his statements were his goals as a painter?



    What formal qualitiies distinguish his work?



3. List two features of Courbet's *Burial at Ornans* (FIG. 21-2) that horrified contemporary critis:

    a.

    b.

How does the work differ from contemporary Romantic works?

4.  In what type of subject matter did Millet specialize?

How was his work viewed by members of the French Middle class?

5.  Although Daumier did many fine paintings, he is primarily known for his

work in the medium of ___________________.

With what type of suject matter was he primarily concerned?

6.  *Le Déjeuner sur l'herbe* (FIG. 21-7), the painting that caused such a scandal at

the Salon des Refusés of 1863, was painted by _______________________

Which aspects of the picture shocked the public?

What was the artist's major concern when he painted the work?

7.  What did the public think that *Olympia* (FIG. 21-8) depicted?

What technical features contributed to Manet's perceived "audacity"?

8.  In what way do the classical figures painted by Bouguereau (FIG. 21-9) differ
from those painted by Manet?

9.  What is meant by the designation "academic art"?

10. What role did the salons play in the artistic life of nineteenth-century France?

11. What earlier style seems to have influenced Rosa Bonheur's *Horse Fair* (FIG. 21-10)?

12. In what style did the American Winslow Homer paint?

13. How did the American public receive Thomas Eakins's *Gross Clinic* (FIG. 21-12)?

14. For what is Eadweard Muybridge most famous?

15. How did Sarget's painting technique differ from that of Eakins?

16. The African-American artist _____________________ studied with Eakins before moving to Paris.  List three characteristics of his style:

    a.

    b.

    c.

17. List two concerns that were shared by the artists who formed the Pre-Raphaelite Brotherhood.

    a.

    b.

18. What is meant by the term "pictorial style" in photography?

19. List four characteristics of Impressionism.

    a.

    b.

    c.

    d.

20. Name four painters who could be consider to be Impressionists.

    a.                              c.

    b.                              d.

21. In what ways does Monet's *Saint-Lazare Train Station* (FIG. 21-21) reflect the new uban Paris?

    In subject matter?

    In style?

22. What is meant by "Hausemanization," and how does Caillebott's *Paris: A Rainy Day* (FIG. 21-22) reflect it?

23. What qualities in photographs like Jouvin's *The Pont Neuf, Paris* (FIG. 21-24) were admired by the Impressionists?

24. What types of subjects did Renoir prefer to paint?

25. Describe one logical discrepancy used by Manet in *A Bar at the Follies-Bergère* (FIG. 21-26) to call attention to the pictorial structure of the painting itself:

26. Define *Japonisme.*

27. In what ways does Degas' work show the influence of photography and of Japanese prints?

    a.

    b.

    c.

28. What stylistic features did Berthe Morisot share with other Impressionists?

29. Which of the Impressionists most systematically investigated the roles of light and color in representing atmosphere and coimage?

    List two devices he used to capture the vibrating quality of light:

    a.

    b.

30. What were Mary Cassatt's favorite subjects?

31. List three influences seen in Toulouse-Lautrec's *At the Moulin Rouge* (FIG. 21-32) and describe the features that reflect each influence.

a.

b.

c.

32. Why did Whistler call his paintings "arrangements" and "nocturnes"?

33. Name four major Post-Impressionist painters, noting the aspects of Impressionism that they criticized and how those criticisms were reflected in their work:

a.

b.

c.

d.

34. For Van Gogh, the primary purpose of color in his paintings was:

35. How did Van Gogh apply paint to his canvas, and what type of effect did his application produce?

36. How did Gauguin's use of color differ from Van Gogh's?

37. Where did Gauguin spend the last ten years of his life?

38. The French painter who used the work of color theorists like Chevreul and

Rood to develop a scientifically precise method of applying paint was

___________________.

What technique did he develop for applying color to canvas and what did he call it?

39. Who said, "I want to make of Impressionism something solid and lasting like the art in the museums"?

40. What two roles does color play in Cezanne's paintings?

a.

b.

41. What does the term "avant-garde" mean?

42. By the end of the nineteenth century, what major change had occurred in the artist's vision of reality?

43. What did the Symbolist artists consider to be their primary task?

44. Puvis de Chavannes was admired by members of the Academy because of his

_________________while the avant-garde artists admired him because of his

_______________ and __________________.

45. List three stylistic characteristics of the work of Gustave Moreau.

a.

b.

c.

46. According to Redon, his originality consisted in:

47. The work of Henri Rousseau (FIG. 21-45) can be related to that of the Symbolists through his reliance on dream and fantasy, but his style differes from theirs in the following way:

48. The major themes in the work of Edvard Munch were:

49. What stylistic influences are most evident in the sculpture of Jean-Baptiste Carpeaux?

50. What style did Augustus Saint-Gaudens utilize for his monument to Mrs. Henry Adams (FIG. 21-48)?


51. What concern did Rodin share with the Impressionists?


What concern did he share with Muybridge and Eakins?


52. What did the commisioners of the *Burghers of Calais* (FIG. 21-50) find offensive in the work?


53. In what country did the Arts and Crafts movement originate?


What was the goal of the movement?


What type of objects did its members produce?


54. Name the Scottish artists who practice the ideas of the Arts and Crafts movement:


Write down two adjectives that describe the designs of husband and wife:


a.                                    b.

55. The style that developed out of the ideals of the Arts and Crafts movement was given different names in different countries. Write down what it was called:

in France, Belgium, Holland, England and the United States:

in Germany:

in Spain:

in Italy:

56. What sort of forms were preferred by Art Nouveau artists?


57. List four sources from which Art Nouveau artists drew inspiration:

   a.

   b.

   c.

   d.

58. The English Graphic artist who worked at the intersection of Art Nouveau
    and symbolism was:

59. Briefly describe Gaudi's architectural style.


60. Describe the sensibility associated with the *fin-de-siècle* period:


61. Briefly describe the style of  Gustave Klimt:



    What features did his work share with the works of nineteenth-century
    Symbolist painters?



**OTHER ARCHITECTURE IN THE LATER 19TH CENTURY**
1.  When did Eiffel construct his tower in Paris (FIG. 21-57)?


    For what event?


2.  What event influenced the technique of encasing iron skeletal structure with
    masonry?

3.  What was the importance of the Marshall Field Warehouse (FIG. 21-58)?


4.  Which features of Sullivan's Carson, Pirie, Scott building (FIG. 21-60) demonstrate his famous dictum "form follows function?"


5.  What style most influenced Hunt's *The Breakers* (FIG. 21-61)?


6.  Name the craftsman whose lavish creations reflected the Art Nouveau  style in America:


## DISCUSSION QUESTIONS

1.  Compare Manet's *Le Déjeuner sur l'herbe* (FIG. 21-7) with Giorgione/Titian's *Pastoral Symphony* (FIG. 17-33). In what ways are they similar, and in what ways do they differ? Why do you think the Parisian public was shocked by Manet's work but considered Giorgioni's work to be a classical masterpiece?

2.  What characteristics does Courbet share with the Impressionists and in what ways does his work differ significantly from theirs? Should the Impressionists be considered Realists?

3.  Compare Eakins's *Gross Clinic* (FIG. 21-12) with Rembrant's *Anatomy Lesson of Dr. Tulp* (FIG. 19-44) and Hawes and Southworth's *Early Operation under Ether* (FIG. 20-65). What medium has each used, and how does the medium influence the art work?

4.  Compare the family portraits depicted by Tanner (FIG. 21-15), Sargent (FIG. 21-14),  Kasebier (FIG. 21-19) and Morisot (FIG. 21-28). Discuss the impression each gives of the relationship between the family members and note the formal elements that the artist usedto create that effect.

5.  Compare Cézanne's still life on FIG. 21-41 with Willem Kalf's on FIG. 19-56. Note differences in composition, the treatment of color, painting technique and distortion of form.

6.  Compare Seurat's A *Sunday on La Grande Jatte* (FIG. 21-39) with Renoir's *Le Moulin de la Galette* (FIG. 21-25). What characteristics do the paintings share?

7.  Discuss the main contribution made by each of the major Post-Impressionists. In what ways are their works a continuation of historical artistic traditions?

8.  Compare MacIntosh's Tea Roon (FIG. 21-52) with the sixteenth-century Japanese Tea House in Kyoto (FIG. 27-7). What attitudes do they share toward craftsmanship and design?

9.  Discuss the influence of Japanese woodblock prints on late nineteenth century French painting.  Select from Degas' *Ballet Rehearsal* (FIG. 21-27), Degas' *The Tub* (FIG. 21-30), Cassatt's *The Bath* (FIG. 21-31), Lautrec's *At the Moulin Rouge* (FIG. 21-32), and Gauguin's *The Vision After the Sermon* (FIG. 21-36). What stylistic features did each artist adopt?

10. In what sense is the slogan "form follows function" accurate or inaccurate as a summary description of the majority of today's architecture? For examples in answering this question, consider buildings in your own community.


### LOOKING CAREFULLY DESCRIBING AND ANALYZING

Write at least one page and a half comparing Van Gogh's *Starry Night* (FIG. 21-35) with Monet's *Impression Sunrise* (FIG. 21-20). Here are some ideas that might help you with your analysis, but do not be limited by them.  First describe all the objects and forms that appear in each painting.  Look carefully at the brush strokes of each artist and describe them noting how apparent the brush strokes are and what sorts of patterns they create, the describe the color that each uses, using the terms hue, intensity and contrast. Describe the underlying composition structures used by both artists. Summarize by noting how these factors contribute to the different emotional impact of the two works.

SUMMARY OF 19th-CENTURY BACKGROUND & STYLES

Fill in the following charts as much as possible from memory, then check your answers against the text in Chapters 20 & 21. (Note particularly p. 683 and 733.)

| BACKGROUND: | Historical People, Events, Ideas, etc. |
|---|---|
| | |

| STYLES | STYLISTIC CHARACTERISTICS | ARTISTS |
|---|---|---|
| Romanticism | | |
| Neoclassicism | | |
| Realism | | |
| Impressionism | | |
| Post-Impressionism | | |
| Symbolism | | |
| Art Noveau | | |

| Artist | Typical Examples | Stylistic Characteristics |
|---|---|---|
| Goya<br>Country: | | |
| Gros<br>Country: | | |
| Gericault<br>Country: | | |
| Delacroix<br>Country: | | |
| Ingres<br>Country: | | |
| Turner<br>Country: | | |
| Constable<br>Country: | | |
| Cole<br>Country: | | |
| Friedrich<br>Country: | | |
| Bierstadt<br>Country: | | |
| Church<br>Country: | | |

| Artist | Typical Examples | Stylistic Characteristics |
| --- | --- | --- |
| Corot<br>Country: | | |
| Daumier<br>Country: | | |
| Courbet<br>Country: | | |
| Manet<br>Country: | | |
| Eakins<br>Country: | | |
| Sargent<br>Country: | | |
| Tanner<br>Country: | | |
| Leibl<br>Country: | | |
| Rosetti<br>Country: | | |
| Millais<br>Country: | | |
| Bouguereau<br>Country: | | |

| Artist | Typical Examples | Stylistic Characteristics |
|---|---|---|
| Bonheur<br>Country: | | |
| Monet<br>Country: | | |
| Caillebotte<br>Country: | | |
| Pissarro<br>Country: | | |
| Renoir<br>Country: | | |
| Degas<br>Country: | | |
| Morisot<br>Country: | | |
| Cassatt<br>Country: | | |
| Toulouse-<br>Latrec<br>Country: | | |
| Whistler<br>Country | | |
| Van Gogh<br>Country: | | |

| Artist | Typical Examples | Stylistic Characteristics |
| --- | --- | --- |
| Gauguin<br>Country: | | |
| Seurat<br>Country: | | |
| Cezanne<br>Country: | | |
| Puvis de<br>Chavannes<br>Country: | | |
| Moreau<br>Country: | | |
| Redon<br>Country: | | |
| Rousseau<br>Country: | | |
| Beardsley<br>Country: | | |
| Klimt<br>Country: | | |

# SUMMARY OF 19<sup>th</sup>-CENTURY PHOTOGRAPHY  (Chapters 20 & 21)

| | Typical Examples | Stylistic Characteristics |
|---|---|---|
| Jouvin<br>Country: | | |
| Daguerre<br>Country: | | |
| Durieu<br>Country: | | |
| Nadar<br>Country: | | |
| Hawes&<br>Southworth<br>Country: | | |
| Muybridge<br>Country: | | |
| Cameron<br>Country: | | |
| Käsebier<br>Country: | | |
| O'Sullivan<br>Country: | | |

SUMMARY OF 19$^{th}$-CENTURY SCULPTURE (Chapters 20 & 21)

| Artist | Typical Examples | Stylistic Characteristics |
|---|---|---|
| Canova<br>Country: | | |
| Lewis<br>Country: | | |
| Rude<br>Country: | | |
| Barye<br>Country: | | |
| Carpeaux<br>Country: | | |
| Saint-<br>Gaudens<br>Country: | | |
| Rodin<br>Country: | | |

<u>SUMMARY OF 19<sup>th</sup>-CENTURY ARCHITECTURE & DESIGN</u> (Chapters 20 & 21)

| | Typical Examples | Stylistic Characteristics |
|---|---|---|
| Vigon<br>Country: | | |
| Barry &<br>Pugin<br>Country: | | |
| Nash<br>Country: | | |
| Garnier<br>Country: | | |
| Labrouste<br>Country: | | |
| Paxton<br>Country: | | |
| W. Morris<br>Country: | | |
| Mackintosh<br>Country: | | |
| Horta<br>Country: | | |
| Gaudi<br>Country: | | |
| Eiffel<br>Country: | | |

| | Typical Examples | Stylistic Characteristics |
| --- | --- | --- |
| Richardson Country: | | |
| Sullivan Country: | | |
| R. Morris Country: | | |
| Tiffany Country: | | |

# 22

# THE DEVELOPMENT OF MODERNIST ART
## THE EARLY 20TH CENTURY

**TEXT PAGES 734-803**

1. A number of scientists, psychlogists, writers and politicians were instrumental in changing our view of the world from the Enlightenment belief in a mechanistic universe o the belief that reason and knowledge would lead to progress and the moral impovement of humanity.  Match the individual on the left with the brief description of their work on the right.

_____ Max Planck            1. Wrote *Interpretation of Dreams*

_____ Charles Darwin        2. Developed Quantum theory

_____ Albert Einstein       3. Theory that survival of the fittest was basis of evolution

_____ Sigmund Freud         4. Advocated collective unconscious

_____ Carl Jung             5. Lead Bolshevik revolution

_____ V. I. Lenin           6. Described matter as another form of energy

_____ Karl Marx             7. Philosopher who held that god is dead

_____ Friedrich Nietzsche   8. Champion of working classes, wrote *Das Capital*

2. How have the discoveries of modern science affected our view of reality?

3.  Give the approximate dates for the folowing significant twentieth-century
    events that influenced art as well as the rest of society:

    World War I:

    Russian Revolution:

    The Great Depression:

    World War II:

4.  List two general directions taken by avant-garde artists in response to the
    turmoil:

    a.

    b.


## EXPRESSIONISM IN EARLY 20th-CENTURY EUROPE

1.  What is meant by the term "Expressionism"?


2.  List three movements classified as expressionist:

    a.                          b.                          c.


3.  In what year was the exhibition held in which the name "Fauve" was
    coined?

    What did it mean?


4.  Name two Fauve painters.

    a.                                          b.

    Describe the characteristics that Fauve paintings have in common.

5.  Name two artists who belonged to *Die Brücke* (The Bridge).

a.                                                                    b.

Why did they select the name *Die Brücke?* What did it signify?

Name three sources for their art.

a.

b.

c.

6.  What beliefs were shared by members of the Blue Rider *(Die Blau Reiter)* group?

Name two artists who belonged to this group.

a.                                                                    b.

7.  Who was Gertrude Stein and what was her significance for the avant-garde of Paris?

Who painted a famous portrait of her?

8.  Identify three probable sources of the dislocation of form seen in Picasso's *Demoiselles d'Avignon* (FIG. 22-9).

a.

b.

c.

9.  Name two Cubist painters.

a.                                      b.


10. What idea did the Cubists adopt from Cézanne?


11. What is the basis of Cubist pictorial space, and how does it differ from
    Renaissance perspective?


12. What is Orphism and who was its founder?


13. How does Synthetic Cubism differ from Analytic Cubism?


14. What is a collage?


15. Name three sculptors whose abstracted froms derive from the experiments
    of the Cubists:

a.                          b.                          c.


16. What new material and technique did Julio Gonzalez contribute to modern
    sculpture?


17. How did Fernand Leger modify Cubist practices?

18. What were the Futurists trying to express in their art?

19. Name two Futurist painters:

   a.                                b.

   Name one Futurist sculptor:

## CHALLENGING ARTISTIC CONVENTIONS

1.  How did the attitude of the Dadaists toward war differ from that of the Futurists:

2.  What was the original purpose of the Dada movement?

   Although short-lived, Dadaism had important consequences for later art. What
   were they?

3.  Name four artists connected with the Dada movement.

   a.                                b.

   c.                                d.

4.  How did Jean Arp utilize chance in his work?

5.  What is a readymade?

   Who developed them?

6.  Describe a "photomontage."


Who developed the technique?


7.  What did Schwitters mean by the term *merz*?


**TRANSATLANTIC ARTISTIC DIALOGUES**
1.  Who were the Eight and what type of painting did they do?


2.  Where and when was the Armory show held and what was its significance?


3.  Name an influenctial work that was exhibited at the Armory show which particularly shocked the public:

What was so upsetting about it?


4.  Who was the founder of the Photo-Secession group and Gallery 291?

What  type of photography did he practice?


5.  The American photographer who was interested in photographic abstraction was:


6.  In what way did the work of Man Ray express the ideas of Dada?

7.  Name two American artists who were influenced by Cubism:

a.                                    b.

8.  What was the Harlem Renaissance?

9.  List two traits shared by the so-called Precisionists, one thematic, one
stylistic:

a.

b.

Name two artists who are considered Precisonists:

a.                                    b.

10. Although the artist___________________________ was first associated with the
Precisionists in New York,  she is best known for her work in New Mexico.

Two of her favorite subjects were _________________ and

_______________.

Describe her style:

**EUROPEAN ART IN THE WAKE OF WORLD WAR  I**
1.  What was the purpose of *Neue Sachlichkeit* artists?

List three artists associated with the movement:

a.                              b.                              c.

2.  For what type of subject is George Grosz most famous?


3.  List three adjectives that describe the style of Max Beckmann:

    a.                              b.                              c.

4.  What mood did Otto Dix create in his *War Triptych*  (FIG. 22-40)?



    What stylistic characteristics help to create the mood?



5.  In what medium did Käthe Kollwitz do most of her work?


    What social class did she most often depict?



6.  List two German Expressionist sculptors.

    a.                              b.

7.  According to Andre Breton, what was the purpose of the Surrealist movement?



8.  Who was the major practitioner of the style known as *pittura metafisica*?


    Describe the mood created with works like the one shown in FIG. 22-44:

9. Name three painters connected with the Surrealist movement, and note what makes their work distinct.

   a.



   b.



   c.



10. What materials did Oppenheim combine in *Object* represented on FIG. 22-48?


11. What type of subject matter did Frida Kahlo prefer?


12. List two techniques used by Surrealist artists to free their creative processes.

   a.

   b.


13. Many artists share the surrealist interest in fanasy, even though they were not formally associated with the group.  However, Andre referred to one of them as "the most Surrealist of us all." To whom did he refer?


14. Who said "Art does not reproduce the visible; rather it makes visible"?


   What did this artist mean by that statement?

15. List three styles that Marc Chagall synthesized in his work.

   a.                          b.                          c.

   What type of subject matter did he draw upon?


## NEW ART FOR A NEW SOCIETY – UTOPIAN IDEALS

1.  What did Malevich believe to be the supreme reality?


   What type of forms did he use to express that reality?


2.  An outstanding representative of the Constructivist movement
   was:


   Why did he call himself a "Constructivist"?


3.  List three new materials used by Naum Gabo.

   a.                          b.                          c.


4.  What did Vladimir Tatlin believe was the purpose of art?


5.  What basic colors and forms characterize Mondrian's mature
   work?


   What did they symbolize for him?


6.  Who designed the Schröder House (FIG. 22-56)?

What style does it reflect?

7.  What was the Bauhaus?

Who founded it?

Name three artists who taught there.

a.                          b.                          c.

8.  What did Moholy-Nagy mean by "vision in motion"?

9.  Who created a series called *Homage to the Square,* and what issues did the series explore?

10. Summarize Gropius' design principles that were incorporated into the Bauhaus?

a.

b.

c.

d.

10. Name a designer and a craftsman who taught at the Bauhaus noting the type of work done by each:

a.

b.


11. List three characteristics of Mies van der Rohe's architectural style that are found in International Style architecture.

   a.

   b.

   c.


   What did Mies van der Rohe mean by "less is more"?


12. Why was the Bauhause closed and who closed it?


   What effect did its closure have on the spread of Bauhaus design principles?


13. What did the Nazis consider to be "degenerate art"?


14. Who defined a house as a "machine for living"?


15. How does Courbusier's Villa Savoye (FIG. 22-64) differ from Wright's houses (FIGS. 22-66 to 22-68)?

16. List four stylistic characteristics of the Art Deco style:

a.

b.

c.

d.


Name one building that illustrates the style:


## EMPHASIZING THE ORGANIC

1.  How was Frank Lloyd Wright's concern for "organic" form reflected in his
    buildings?

    List two houses he designed:   a.                                    b.

2.  What type of form did Brancusi believe was "the most real"?



3.  What do the sculpture of Brancusi and Barbara Hepworth's have
    in common?



4.  List three characteristics of the sculpture of Henry Moore.

    a.

    b.

    c.

    What was the most recurrent theme in his work?


    What apparently originally inspired it?

5.  What is a mobile?


## ART AS POLITICAL STATEMENT IN THE 1930s

1.  What event inspired Picasso's *Guernica* (FIG. 22-73)?


    What symbols did Picasso use to refer to the event, and how did he
    emphasize its horror?




2.  What is the political significance of Vera Mukhina's sculpture shown on FIG.
    22-74?



3.  What was the WPA, and what was its effect on the arts?




4.  The American woman photographer whose work brought the nation's
    attention to the plight of the rural poor was:


5.  What is the dominant mood of Hopper's *Nighthawks* (FIG. 22-76)?


6.  What was the favorite subject of Jacob Lawrence?

7.  Name two American artists who were associated with the Regionalist School:

    a.                               b.

    What type of subjects did they paint?



8.  What was the theme of much of Orozco's work?



    In what medium did he do most of his work?



9.  Why did Diego Rivera want to work in a simple, easily accessible style?

    List three aspects of that style:

    a.

    b.

    c.


## EMIGRES AND EXILES: ENERGIZING AMERICAN ART AT MID CENTURY

Name twelve European artists who came to America because of the political chaos of Europe during World War II:

|       |       |       |       |
|-------|-------|-------|-------|
| a.    | b.    | c.    | d.    |
| e.    | f.    | g.    | h.    |
| i.    | j.    | k.    | l.    |

1. Compare the use of mass, space, and decorative detail in the Villa Rotonda (FIG. 17-56), Blenheim (FIG. 19-75), Chiswick House (FIG. 20-27), the Villa Savoye (FIG. 22-64), and the Kaufmann House (FIG. 22-68). Which do you like best? Why?

2. Relate Maurice Denis's statement that "a picture before being a war horse, a nude woman, or some anecdote, is essentially a plane surface covered with colors assembled in a certain order" to the early twentieth-century paintings you have studied. How does his view differ from the traditional one regarding the meaning and purpose of a painting? Which artists do you think would agree with Maurice Denis? Why?

3. In what ways does the work of Kollwitz (FIG. 22-41), Barlach (FIG. 22-43), Dix (FIG. 22-40), and Beckmann (FIG. 22-39), relate to eachother? Do you think there are any consistent "German" characteristics?

4. Discuss Picasso's statement "I paint forms as I think them, not as I see them." How does the Cubist conception of space differ from that held during the Renaissance?

5. Concern with social issues is apparent in the work of many twentieth century artists, including Mukhina (FIG. 22-74), Lawrence (FIG. 22-77), Beckmann (FIG. 22-39), Kollwitz (FIG. 22-41), Lange (FIG. 22-75), Orozco (FIG. 22-80), Tatlin (FIG. 22-54), and Barlach (FIG. 22-43). Identify the issue that was addressed in each work and the stylistic means the artist used to express that concern. Which do you think is most effective?

6. Compare Brancusi's *Bird in Space* (FIG. 22-69) with Gabo's *Column* (FIG. 22-53). In what ways are the forms similar, and in what ways are they different? How does each artist explain the techniques and goals of his art?

7. Discuss the role of chance in both the Dada and Surrealist movements. What connection do you see between the Dada movement and art movements today?

8. Discuss the aesthetic that developed at the Bauhaus, selecting five images done by Bauhaus faculty to illustrate your discussion. What effects of their influence do you see in contemporary life?

<h1 style="text-align:center">LOOKING CAREFULLY, DESCRIBING AND ANALYZING</h1>

Look carefully at two 20th-century depictions of war, one by Otto Dix, shown on FIG. 22-40, the other by Picasso on FIG. 22-73, and write at least one page analyzing and comparing them. Use the following terms: size and scale: form and composition; material and technique; line and color; mass and volume, picture plane and distortion. Here are some questions that might help you with your analysis, but do not be limited by them.

First look at the shape, size and scale of each image. In what way to these relate to earlier images? Which image seems to be most traditional? What type of composition does each use? Examine each of the panels in the Dix image and describe what you see in each. Describe each of the figures in the Picasso and note how they are related to each other. How does each artist handle space and the picture plane? What war is each depicting? What distortions does each artist use to express the horror of the events? Which do you think is most effective?

# 23

# FROM THE MODERN TO THE POSTMODERN AND BEYOND
## ART OF THE LATER 20TH CENTURY

**TEXT PAGES  804-865**

**THE ART WORLD'S FOCUS SHIFTS WEST**

1.  List two characteristics of so-called "Greenbergian formalism":

2.  Why is it difficult to give a precise definition of the term "Postmodernism"?

    In contrast to Modernism, which may be considered to be elitist,
    Postmodernism is:

3.  What is the attitude of Existentialists toward human existence?

    List three artists whose work reflects these ideas:

    a.                          b.                          c.

4.  Name the artist who referred to his art as "an attempt to remake the violence
    of reality itself":

5.  List two characteristics of the art of Jean Dubuffet:

    a.

    b.

6.  What is Art Brut?

7.  In what way does the sculpture of Giacometti, like the figure shown on FIG. 23-3, relate to the ideas of the Existentialists?


## MODERNIST FORMALISM

1.  What major artistic style developed in the United States after the influx of refugee artists from Europe?

    In what city did it begin?


2.  Describe the way Jackson Pollock created his "gestural" Abstract Expressionist pieces.


3.  List one way in which de Kooning's work relates to that of Pollack:

    List one way in which it differs:


4.  What do the works of Barnett Newman and Mark Rothko have in common?


5.  Describe the function of Barnett Newman's "zips."


6.  What feelings did Mark Rothko hope to evoke with his large, luminous canvases?


7.  How does Post-Painterly Abstraction differ from Abstract Expressionism?


8.  Why was Ellsworth Kelly's work known as "Hard Edge Abstraction"?

9.  What is Color-Field painting?


10. Describe Frankenthaler's soak-stain technique.



What effect did she want to achieve with it?


Name one other artist who utilized it:


11. Name three Minimalist sculptors:

a.                              b.                              c.


12. In what way are the principles of Post-Painterly Abstraction related to
Minimalist sculpture?



13. What beliefs about art did Donald Judd assert in works like the cubes
illustrated in FIG. 23-15?



14. Briefly describe the Vietnam Memorial in Washington D.C. (FIG. 23-16):

Who designed it?

Why do you think visitors respond to it so strongly?



15. In what way did David Smith's sculpture like the one on FIG. 23-9 differ
from Minimalist works?

16. What type of art did Louise Nevelson create?


17. How does the work of Louise Bourgeois' Post-Minimalist work differ from the work of Judd and other artists of the Minimalist school?



18. What is a "Happening"?


   Name one artist who specialized in Happenings.


19. Who was John Cage?



20. What type of art did Fluxus artists create?



21. What sort of art was produced by Kazno Shirago and the Gutac group in Oasaka?



22. Briefly state the artistic philosophy of Joseph Beuys.



23. What inspired the work of Jean Tinguely, and what sort of materials did he use?

24. What is meant by "Conceptual Art"?


25. What was Bruce Nauman's favorite material?


What was his favorite subject?

## ART FOR THE PUBLIC

1.  What subject matter was characteristic of Pop Art of the 1960s?


2.  Name two artists who worked in the Pop mode in England.

    a.                                b.


3.  Give an example of Jasper Johns' "things seen but not looked at:"


4.  What are "combine" paintings?


    Who developed them?


5.  What distinguishes the works of Robert Rauschenberg from those of earlier
    Dada artists?


6.  What did Lichtenstein utilize as the basis of works like the one shown on
    FIG. 23-30?


    How do his "benday dots" reflect the source?

7.  How did Andy Warhol utilize his background as a commercial artist in creating "fine art" works?


8.  Name the artist who created designs for gigantic monuments  depicting ordinary objects:


9.  Name two Superrealist painters:

    a.                                      b.


10. What type of art did Duane Hanson create?


11. Name the leading American Environmental artist:

    Briefly describe his techniques.


12. For what type of art are Christo and his wife Jeane-Claude most famous?


13. Why did the GSA remove Serra's *Tilted Arc* (FIG. 23-39) from the plaza in front of the Federal Building in New York City?


    What important issues were raised by this action?

**NEW MODELS FOR ARCHITECTURE: MODERNISM TO POSTMODERNISM**

1.  What form did Frank Lloyd Wright use as the basis for his design for the Guggenheim Museum (FIGS. 23-40 and 23-41)?

2.  What forms provided the inspiration for Le Corbusier's Notre Dame du
    Haut (FIGS. 23-42 and 23-43)



    In what way does Notre Dame du Haut differ from Le Corbusier's earlier
    works (FIGS. 22-63 and 22-64)?


3.  List two architectural metaphors used in the Opera House in Sydney
    Australia (FIG. 23-44):

    a.

    b.


4.  Who designed the TWA Terminal at Kennedy Airport in New York City
    (FIG. 23-45):

    What design motif did he use throughout the structure?


5.  What architectural style is represented by the Seagram Building in New York
    (FIG. 23-46)?


6.  What type of impression was the Sears Tower in Chicago (FIG. 23-47)
    intended to project?

    What features of the building helped to create that impression?


7.  List three terms often associated with Postmodern architecure:

    a.                          b.                          c.


8.  What historical styles are cited by Charles Moore in his *Piazza d'Italia* (FIG.
    23-48)?

9.  How did Phillip Johnson's style change in his AT&T Tower in New York (FIG. 23-49)?


10. What aspects of Graves' Portland Building (FIG. 23-50) can be considered Postmodernist?


11. How did Lionel Venturi's work and writing depart from the Modernist axiom "form follows function"?


12. What is the official name for the "Beaubourg"?


    Where is it located?


    What is significant about its structure?


13. What is meant by Deconstructionism?


14. List six adjectives that describe Deconstructivist architecture:

    a.                                      b.

    c.                                      d.

    e.                                      f.

    Name a building that illustrates those terms:


## POSTMODERNISM IN PAINTING, SCULPTURE AND NEW MEDIA

1.  Give one way that Postmodern artists challenge the Modernist emphasis on originality and creativity:

2.  Jameson argues that the intersection of high and mass culture is a defining feature of:


3.  In rejecting the notion that each art work contains a fixed meaning,

    Postmodern artists are influenced by the ideas of _________________theorists.


4.  Briefly characterized the style of Julian Schnabel:



    His work has been considered as a restatement of the_________________
    style.

5.  Why is Susan Rothenberg characterized as a Neo-Expressionist?



6.  What theme is seen in many of Anselm Kiefer's works?



7.  Why did Ofili's *Holy Virgin Mary* (FIG. 23-58) elicit such a strong reaction?



8.  Name two artists who consider themselves to be feminist artists.

    a.                              b.


9.  Who designed *The Dinner Party* (FIG. 23-59)?



    What was it designed to celebrate?


    What techniques were used to create it?

10. For what type of art is Miriam Shapiro most famous?


   What did she mean by the name "femmage"?


11. Who produced a series of film stills in which she transformed herself (FIG. 23-61)?


   What issue was of primary concern to the artist?


12. To what issues does Barbara Kruger want her art to draw attention?


13. Name the artist whose works constituted "a dialogue between the landscape and the female body"?


   What feelings do her works evoke?


14. What issue is of major concern to Kiki Smith?


15. Name three artists who used their art to explore issues involved with being African American women:

   a.                          b.                          c.

16. What issue did Melvin Edwards explore in works like *Tambo* (FIG. 23-69)?


17. Name a Native American artist who uses cultural heritage and historical references to comment on the present:

18. List three stylistic features of Leon Golub's art that characterize his brutal vision of contemporary life:

a.

b.

c.

19. What medium does Magdalena Abakanowicz use for her expressive sculptures?

20. What subject was David Wojnarowicz exploring in the work shown on FIG. 23-74?

21. What artistic technique did Wodiczko utilize to draw attention to the plight of the homeless?

22. List six interests that video technology allowed Nam Jujne Paik to combine:

a.                              b.

c.                              d.

e.                              f.

23. Name four artists who utilize computers and/or video in their work:

a.                              b.

c.                              d.

Which one uses digital video to encourage introspection and explore spirituality?

24. What is Jeff Koons exploring in works like *Pink Panther* (FIG. 23-81)?

25. How does Tansey's *A Short History of Modernist Painting* (FIG. 23-82) illustrate the ambiguities and paradoxes of Postmodernist Pictorialism?


26. To what was Arneson reacting in his self-portrait known as *California Artist* (FIG. 23-83):


In what way is the work a critique of the contemporary art world?


27. What is Hans Haake critiquing in *MetroMobiltan* (FIG. 23-84)?


28. Who are the Guerrilla Girls, and what is their agenda?


## DISCUSSION QUESTIONS

1.  What European political events and artistic movements influenced the development of American Abstract Expressionism? How?

2.  Discuss the use of industrial processes in the work of David Smith, Julio Gonzalez, and Donald Judd. Which processes did each use and how were the processes related to the artist's esthetic concerns?

3.  Compare Hamilton's *Just What Is It That Makes Today's Homes So Different, So Appealing?* (FIG. 23-27) with Campin's *Merode Altarpiece* (FIG. 15-12). Discuss the compositional structure and the symbolism of both works, along with their cultural meanings.

4.  Can you relate Judd's *Untitled* (FIG. 23-15) and Tinguely's *Homage to New York* (FIG. 23-24) , and Sherman's *Untitled Film Still #35* (FIG. 23-61) to the earlier traditions of Classic and Romantic art? How?

5.  Compare the self-portraits of Cindy Sherman (FIG. 23-61), Ana Mendieta (FIG. 23-63), Adrian Piper (FIG. 23-67),  Chuck Close (FIG. 23-35), and Robert Arneson (FIG. 23-83) with earlier self-portraits like those of Judith Leyster (FIG. 19-49), Vigee-Lebrun (FIG. 20-13)  and Rembrandt (FIG. 19-47). Discuss the techniques used by each artist as well as the view of the self that each presents.

6. Compare Francis Bacon's *Painting* (FIG. 23-1) and David Wojnarowicz's "When I put my hands on your body" (FIG. 23-74). What attitudes toward society does each represent, and how is each reflective of its time?

7. If you have Volume I, discuss the changes in still life depiction from the time of the Romans through the modern day. Select from the *Still Life with Peaches* from Herculaneum (FIG. 7-24), Claes, *Vanitas Still Life* (FIG. 19-55), Cezanne, *The Basket of Apples* (FIG. 21-41), Picasso's *Still Life with Chair-caning* (FIG. 22-12), Warhol's *Green Coca-Cola Bottles* (FIG. 23-31), abnd Hanson's *Supermarket Shopper* (FIG. 23-36). What was the purpose of each art work and what techniques did the artists use to achieve those purposes?

8. What changes in social and religious attitudes are represented by the comparison of Puvis de Chavannes, *The Sacred Grove* (FIG. 21-42) , Rothko's *No. 14* (FIG. 23-8), Bill Viola's *The Crossing* (FIG. 23-79), Judy Chicago's *The Dinner Party* (FIG. 23-59), and Chris Ofili *The Holy Virgin Mary* (FIG. 23-58).

9. Recently, the International Style, which has dominated the architecture of the past fifty years, seems to have fallen into disfavor. What criticisms have been leveled against it? In your opinion, are they justified? Describe some of the alternatives that have been tried.

10. One reason for the stylistic similarity of International Style buildings, whether erected in Brasilia, Tokyo, Paris, or New York, is the architects' dependence upon intricate machinery to control the interior climates of their buildings. Do you feel that increasing reliance on complex technology is still justified in view of dwindling energy sources and the threat of accompanying economic and social upheavals throughout the world? What practical alternatives, if any, do you see?

## LOOKING CAREFULLY, ANALYZING AND RELATING

Look carefully at the representations of two late 20th century high tech buildings: Rogers and Piano's Pompidou Center (FIG. 23-52) and Gehry's Guggenheim Bilbao Museo (FIG. 23-54) and write at least a page comparing them. Although they both emphasize the use of modern technology, the effects they create are quite different. How did the use of materials influence the visual effects each produced? Describe each building as fully as you can, and then relate the two buildings to earlier architectural traditions of Classical and Baroque. What earlier buildings might you relate them to? Explain the features that made you think of the relationship.

SUMMARY OF 20$^{\text{TH}}$-CENTURY ART MOVEMENTS

Fill in the following charts as much as possible from memory, then check your answers against the text in Chapters 22 & 23. (Note particularly pp. 803 & 865)

| | Artists | Stylistic Characteristics | Historical Factors |
| --- | --- | --- | --- |
| **EXPRESSIONISM** Country: | | | |
| **FAUVISM** Country: | | | |
| **CUBISM** Country: | | | |
| **PURISM** Country: | | | |
| **FUTURISM** Country: | | | |
| **DADA** Country: | | | |
| **INTERNATIONAL STYLE** Countries: | | | |

|  | Artists | Stylistic Characteristics | Historical Factors |
| --- | --- | --- | --- |
| **ARMORY SHOW** Country: |  |  |  |
| **PRECISIONISM** Country: |  |  |  |
| **NEUSACHLIKEIT** Country: |  |  |  |
| **SURREALISM** Country: |  |  |  |
| **PITTURA METAFISICA** Country: |  |  |  |
| **SUPREMATISM** Country: |  |  |  |
| **CONSTRUCTIVISM** Country: |  |  |  |

|  | Artists | Stylistic Characteristics | Historical Actors |
|---|---|---|---|

**DE STIJL**
Country:

**BAUHAUS**
Country:

**ORGANIC SCULPTURE**

**SOCIAL CONCERNS**

**REGIONALISM**
Country:

**MEXICAN MURALISTS**

**ABSTRACT EXPRESSIONISM**
Country:

SUMMARY OF 20$^{\text{TH}}$-CENTURY ART MOVEMENTS (Continued)

|  | Artists | Stylistic Characteristics | Historical Actors |
|---|---|---|---|
| **POST-WAR EXPRESSIONISM** Countries: |  |  |  |
| **POST-PAINTERLY ABSTRACTION** Country: |  |  |  |
| **MINIMALISM** |  |  |  |
| **PERFORMANCE ART** |  |  |  |
| **CONCEPTUAL ART** |  |  |  |
| **POP ART** Countries: |  |  |  |
| **SUPERREALISM** |  |  |  |

|  | Artists | Stylistic Characteristics | Historical Actors |
|---|---|---|---|
| **EARTH & SITE ART** |  |  |  |
| **POSTMODERNISM** |  |  |  |
| **ACTIVIST ART** |  |  |  |
| **FEMINIST ART** |  |  |  |
| **VIDEO & DIGITAL ART** |  |  |  |

SUMMARY OF TWENTIETH-CENTURY ARCHITECTS
Fill in the following charts as much as possible from memory, then check your answers
against the text in Chapter 22 and 23.

|  | Typical Examples | Stylistic Characteristics |
| --- | --- | --- |
| **RIETVELD**<br>Country: |  |  |
| **GROPIUS**<br>Country: |  |  |
| **MIES VAN**<br>**DER ROHE**<br>Country: |  |  |
| **LE CORBUSIER**<br>Country: |  |  |
| **WRIGHT**<br>Country: |  |  |
| **VAN ALEN**<br>Country: |  |  |
| **UTZON**<br>Country: |  |  |
| **SAARINEN**<br>Country: |  |  |

| | Typical Examples | Stylistic Characteristics |
|---|---|---|
| SKIDMORE OWINGS & MERRIL<br>Country: | | |
| MOORE<br>Country: | | |
| JOHNSON & BURGEE<br>Country: | | |
| GRAVES<br>Country: | | |
| VENTURI<br>Country: | | |
| ROGERS & PIANO<br>Country: | | |
| BENNISCH<br>Country: | | |
| GEHRY<br>Country: | | |

PREPARING FOR YOUR EXAMINATIONS.

As you prepare to take your examination you should review the notes you took on your lectures as well as the work you did in your Study Guide.   (Look back at the **Introduction to the Study Guide** for tips on taking notes and creating your own charts, as well as detailed instructions on studying for and taking examinations.) If you have not yet filled out the Summary charts in the Guide, this is the time to do it, integrating materials from your lecture notes with materials in the Guide itself. This activity is the most useful thing that you can do.

The self-quiz included below as well as the materials included in the **ArtStudy** CD and the **Companion Site** for the textbook http://art.wadsworth.com/gardnerwestern12 can be a great help in preparing you for course examinations. The quiz below includes types of questions often asked in art history exam examinations: multiple choice, short answer questions, chronology exercises, essay questions and attribution of unknown images. So take the self-quiz and check your answers in the back of the book so that you can see how well you grasp the material.

# Self-Quiz

# EARLY MODERN: RENAISSANCE & BAROQUE

**CHAPTERS 14-19**

MULTIPLE CHOICE

Circle the most appropriate answer.

1. Which of the following architects best exemplifies the principles of High Renaissance style?

    a. Guarini
    b. Bramante
    c. Brunelleschi
    d. Borromini
    e. Michelozzo

2. Which of the following Dutch artists specialized in landscape?

    a. Hals
    b. van Honthorst
    c. van Ruisdael
    d. Kalf
    e. Vermeer

3. A work in the Classical Baroque style would most likely have been created by:

    a. Poussin
    b. Pozzo
    c. Rubens
    d. Velázquez
    e. Bernini

4. The combination of Germanic and Italian characteristics is most apparent in the work of:

    a. Leonardo
    b. Cranach
    c. Bosch
    d. Holbein
    e. Grünewald

5. The counter-positioning of a figure about its central axis with the weight of the body on one leg and the other leg relaxed is called:

    a. chairoscuro
    b. contrapposto
    c. condottiere
    d. antipasto
    e. sfumato

6. Tenebroso refers to:

    a. a small range of tone between light and dark
    b. objects in a painting that have been painted over
    c. the point where orthogonals converge
    d. a technique using violent contrasts of light and dark
    e. an affliction known as "mural painter's elbow"

7. A painting using much gold, flat patterns, a high horizon line, elegant figure style, many details from nature and curvilinear line would most likely be:

a. High renaissance
b. Early Renaissance
c. Mannerism
d. International Gothic
e. Baroque

8. The paintings of Vermeer most often convey a feeling of:

a. agitation
b. ostentation
c. serenity
d. pomposity
e. fury

9. Which of the following artists worked for Francis I at Fontainbleau?

a. Boucher
b. Poussin
c. Le Nain
d. Ruben
e. Rosso

10. In which of the following cities did Borromini build the majority of his buildings?

a. Rome
b. Florence
c. Paris
d. Venice
e. Milan

11. The supreme master of the group portrait was:

a. Hals
b. Steen
c. Gainsborough
d. Anguissola
e. Ghiberti

12. Seventeenth-century Dutch paintings were characteristically:

    a. commissioned by the aristocracy
    b. commissioned by the church
    c. painted to glorify military leaders
    d. sold on the open market
    e. scarce and hard to find

13. Which of the following is *least* characteristic of Baroque art?

    a. dramatic use of light
    b. emphasis on diagonal lines
    c. calm, classical figures
    d. a reflection of the ideals of the counter-Reformation
    e. energy and complexity of design

14. Which is *least* characteristic of Baroque architecture?

    a. three-part division of the facade
    b. preference for rectangular and circular decorative motifs
    c. emphasis on a grand central entrance
    d. greater variation in the depth of wall surface
    e. preference for oval over circular plans

15. The *School of Athens* in the Vatican was painted by:

    a. Leonardo
    b. Raphael
    c. Michelangelo
    d. Bramante
    e. Perugino

16. Which building is located in Paris?

    a. Palazzo vecchio
    b. Campidoglio
    c. Louvre
    d. Farnese palace
    e. Fontainbleu palace

17. Oil painting was first used by the:

    a. fifteenth-century Flemish (Netherlanders)
    b. fifteenth-century Florentines
    c. sixteenth-century Venetians
    d. fifteenth-century Germans
    e. sixteenth-century Germans

18. The *Virgin of the Rocks* illustrates both the scientific and artistic interests of:

    a. Botticelli
    b. Leonardo
    c. Raphael
    d. Dürer
    e. Bellini

19. The innovative frescos of the Arena chapel were painted by:

    a. Masaccio
    b. Michelangelo
    c. Giotto
    d. Duccio
    e. Raphael

20. Which artist was commissioned to design a tomb for Julius II?

    a. Donatello
    b. Verrocchio
    c. Michelangelo
    d. Giovanni da Bologna
    e. Bernini

21. A concern for realism, psychological portraiture, and emotional expression best describes the style of the:

    a. Italian "proto-renaissance"
    b. International Gothic
    c. Italian High Renaissance
    d. German Renaissance
    e. Mannerism

22. Which of the following least characterizes the International Gothic style:

    a. intricate ornamentation
    b. rational perspective
    c. splendid processions
    d. uptilted ground plane
    e. brilliant color and costuming

23. An important characteristic of much fifteenth-century Flemish (Netherlandish) art was the use of:

    a. linear pespective
    b. disguised symbolism
    c. contrapposto
    d. sfumato
    e. painterly brush strokes

24. The use of sfumato, full figures, psychological interpretation, and anatomical accuracy most correctly describes the work of:

    a. Lorenzetti
    b. El Greco
    c. Leonardo
    d. Duccio
    e. Botticelli

25. Which of the following is *not* characteristic of High Renaissance figure painting?

    a. slow, rhythmic movement
    b. rational control
    c. restrained gravity
    d. balance and order
    e. elongaton and distortion

26. Which artist created paintings illustrating the life of peasants?

    a. van Eyck
    b. Holbein
    c. Bruegel
    d. Le Nain
    e. both c and d

27. The Limbourg brothers were known for their:

    a. frescoes
    b. engravings
    c. panel paintings
    d. manuscript illuminations
    e. woodcuts

28. Bout's work is best classified as:

    a. Italian High Renaissance
    b. fifteenth-century Flemish (Netherlandish)
    c. International Gothic
    d. Italian Proto-Renaissance
    e. Mannerist

29. Which of the following Baroque painters did *not* do frescoed ceilings?

    a. Pozzo
    b. Pietro da cortona
    c. Caravaggio
    d. Reni
    e. Annibale Carracci

30. Which of the following architects did not take part in the building of Saint Peter's or its piazza?

    a. Bramante
    b. Michelangelo
    c. Maderna
    d. Bernini
    e. Borromini

## CHRONOLOGY EXERCISE

Write down the letter corresponding to the appropriate <u>Century</u> beside the name of the artist or art work:

| | |
|---|---|
| _____31. Palladio | a. 14th Century |
| _____32. Brunelleschi | b. 15th Century |
| _____33. van der Weyden | c. 16th Century |
| _____34. Velázquez | d. 17th Century |
| _____35. Bernini | e. 18th Century |

____36.  Masaccio

____37.  Assam

____38.  Van Ruisdael

____39.  Bruegel

____40.  Bramante


## STYLISTIC EXERCISE

Write down the letter corresponding to the appropriate <u>Style</u> beside the name of the artist:

____41. Borromini                           a. Northern Renaissance

____42. Donatello                           b. Italian $15^{th}$ c Renaissance

____43. Raphael                             c. Italian High Renaissance

____44. Dürer                               d. Mannerist

____45. Velázquez                           e. Baroque

____46. Memling

____47. Uccello

____48. Parmigianino

____49. Hals

____50. Rembrandt


## GEOGRAPHIC EXERCISE

Indicate the <u>Architect</u> or <u>Artist</u> and the <u>Country</u> where each of the works is found.

| Work | Architect /Artist | Country |
| --- | --- | --- |
| 51. Campidoglio | | |
| 52. Church of Vierzehnheiligen | | |
| 53. Ghent Altarpiece | | |

54. Dome of Florence Cathedral        _________________________        _______________

55. Banqueting Hall, Whitehall        _________________________        _______________

56. San Carlo alle Quattro Fontane    _________________________        _______________

57. Isenheim Altarpiece               _________________________        _______________

58. Ecstasy of St. Theresa            _________________________        _______________

59. Sistine Ceiling                   _________________________        _______________

60. Versailles                        _________________________        _______________


## SHORT ANSWER QUESTIONS

Answer the question or finish the sentence.

61. What is meant by the term "Maniera Graeca"?


62. Where did el Greco do most of his work?  What type of subject matter did he prefer?


63. What is portrayed in Ambrodio Lorenzetti's frescos in Siena, and why are they important?


64. Name three fifteenth-century artists who were very much interested in linear perspective:


65. What features characterize the work of Domenico Ghirlandaio?


66. Who were the greatest patrons of art in fifteenth-century Florence?


67. Describe the difference between aerial and linear perspective:


68. Name one French Renaissance sculptor and characterize his style:


69. How was the work of Cranach associated with the Protestant Reformation?

70. How does Van der Weyden's style differ from that of Van Eyck?


71. In what type of art did Hans Holbein specialize? In what country did he do his best
know works?


72. Name four architects who worked on Saint Peter's in Rome:


73. In what type of painting did Rachael Ruysch specialize?


74. Who was Velázquez's major patron? What country was he from?


75. Briefly describe the characteristics of Caravaggio's style:


76. What is the "Grand Manner"?


77. Name at least one building that demonstrates the principles of the French classical
Baroque style:


78. Name the Baroque artist who is famous for both his sculpture and his architecture.  In
what city did he do most of his work?


79. What type of subject matter was portrayed in a "veduta" painting?


80. Name two English architects who worked in the 17$^{th}$ or 18$^{th}$ centuries:

81. Compare the two pictures of the Virgin Madonna below, attributing each to an artist, country, century, and style. Give the reasons for your attributions.

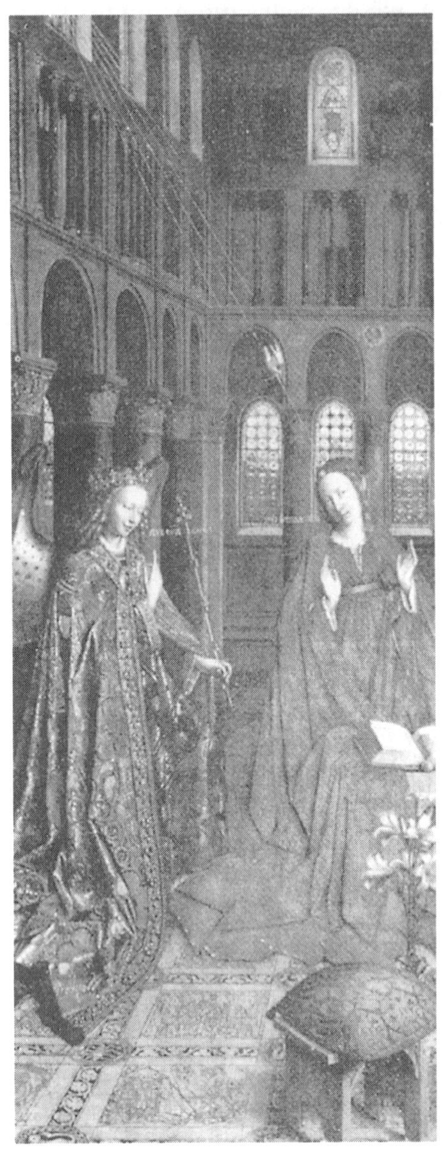

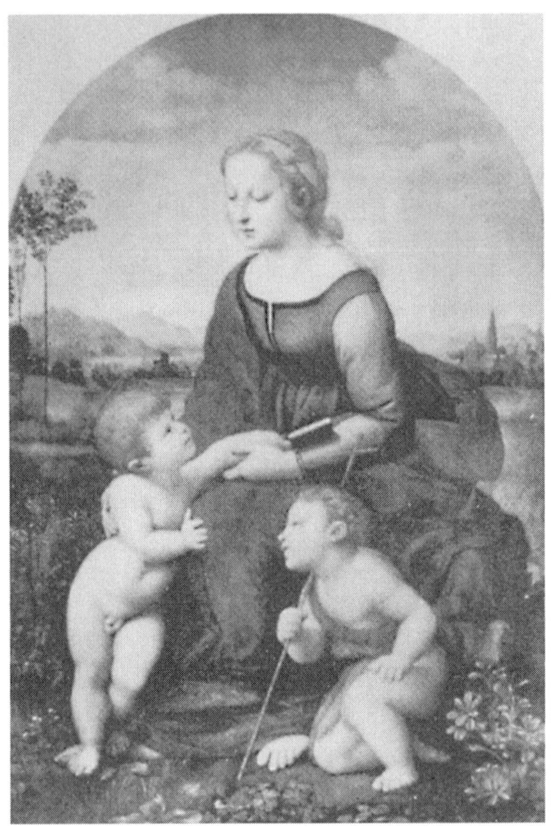

A.  Artist:                          Country:

    Century:                        Style:

    Reasons:

B.  Artist:                          Country:

    Century:                        Style:

    Reasons:

82. Compare the plan and photograph of the building below, attributing it to an artist, country, century, and style. Give the reasons for your attributions.

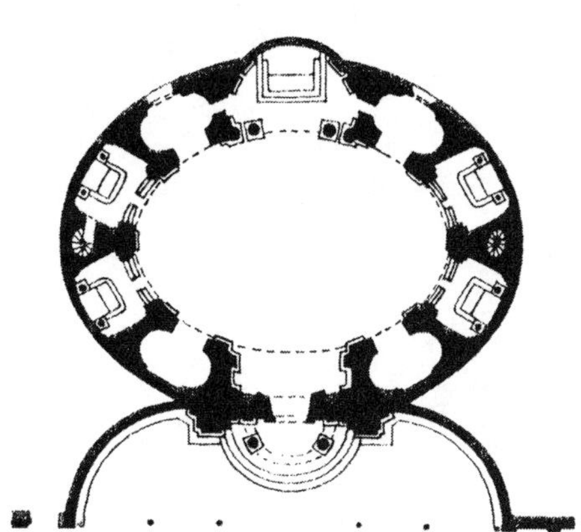

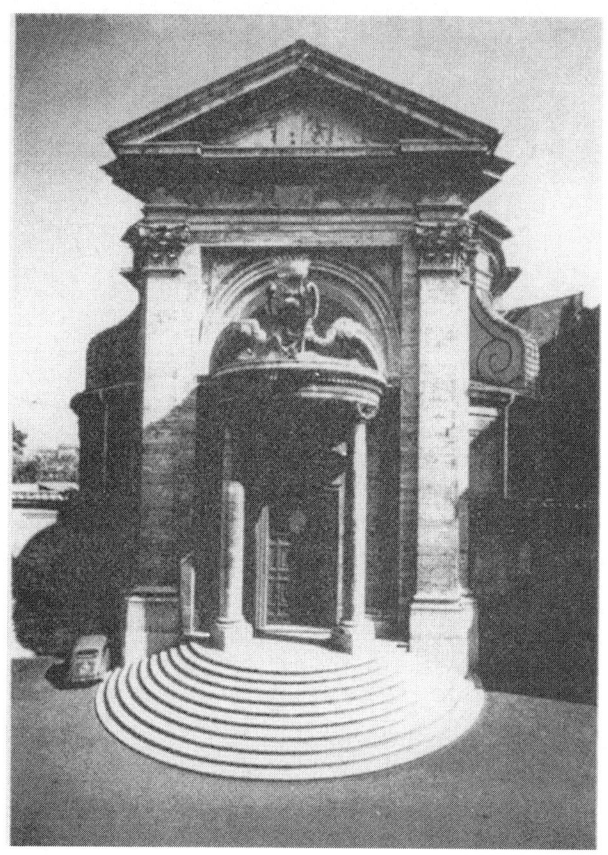

Artist:                                    Century:

Country:                                   Style:

Reasons:

83. These two very different interpretations of the sky were painted in the same century but in different countries. Attribute these paintings to a century and assign a country to each. Describe the artistic concerns that link these paintings to the same period as well as the differences between them. How might these differences have been affected by the patrons for whom the artists worked?

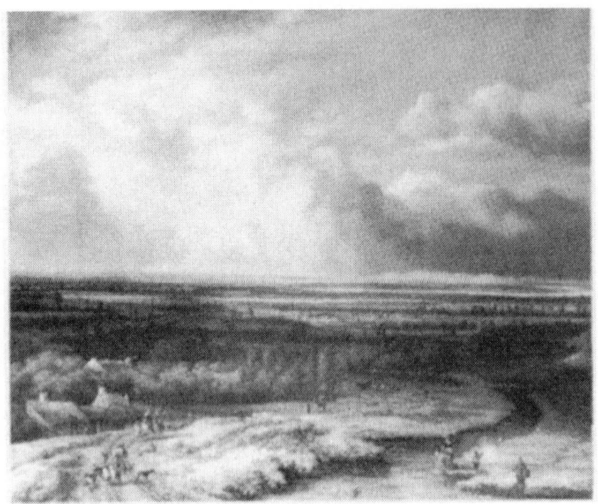

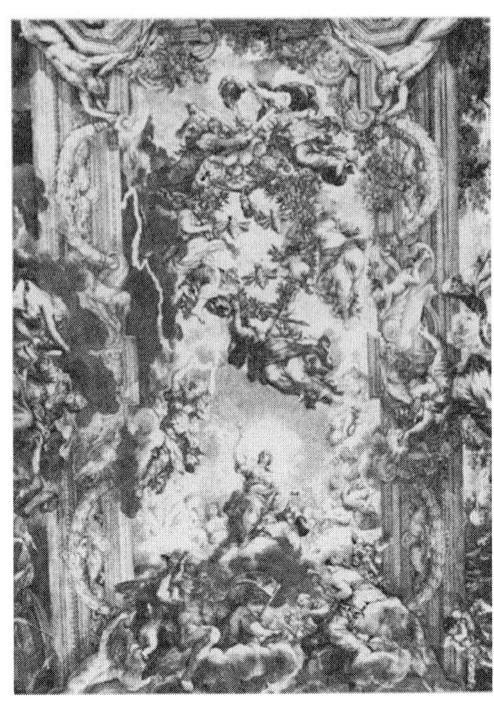

Century:

Country A:

Country B:

84. Compare the two paintings below, attributing each to an artist, country, and century. How do these paintings illustrate the different approaches to the use of light that characterize the works of these two artists?

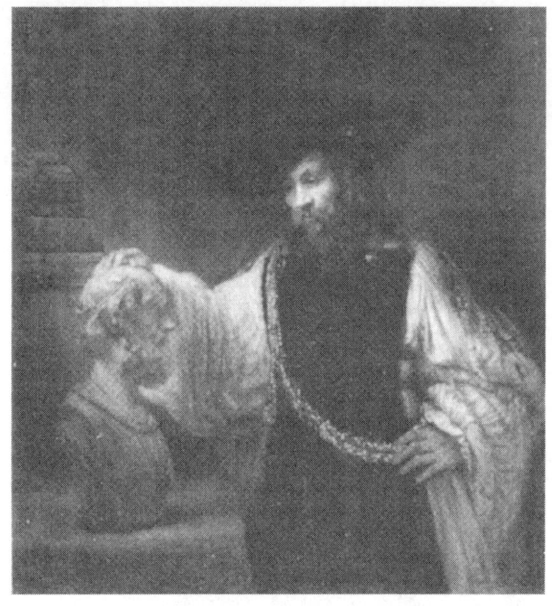 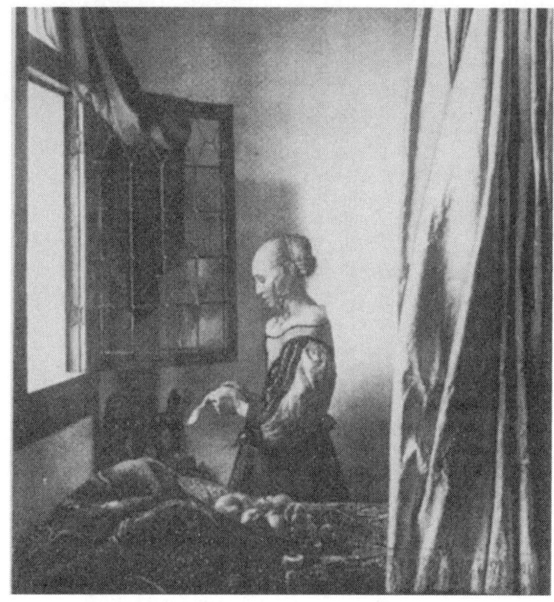

Artist A:                                          Artist B:

Country A:                                         Country B:

Century A:                                         Century B:

85. Compare the two sculptures below, attributing each to an artist, country, century, and style. Give the reasons for your attributions.

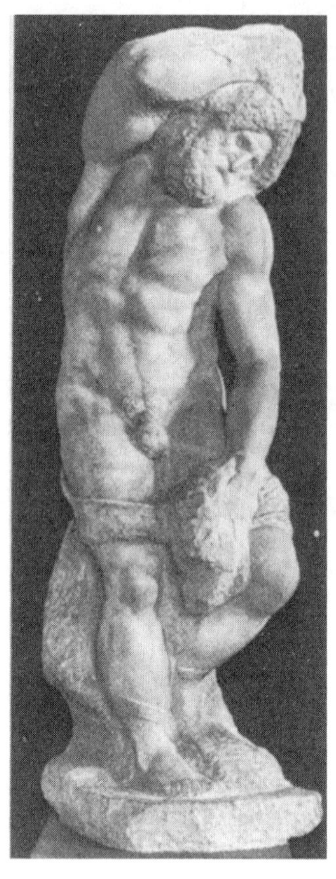 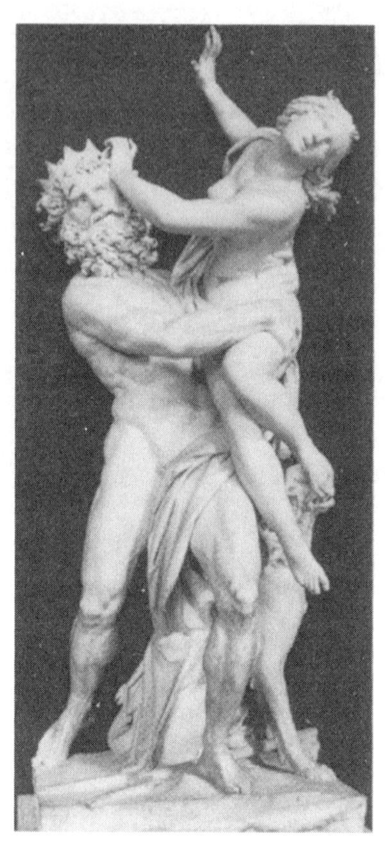

Artist A:                                    Artist B:

Country A:                                   Country B:

Century A:                                   Century B:

Style A:                                     Style B:

Reasons:                                     Reasons:

ESSAYS

Select one essay, and be sure and cite specific examples to illustrate your argument.

1. Compare the development of painting during the 15$^{th}$ century in Florence and the Netherlands.  What were the major concerns and achievements of the two areas? Select two or three artists to illustrate your argument, citing specific works.

2. Discuss patronage during the 17$^{th}$ century in Europe. Note the different types of patrons that were found in Italy, Holland, Belgium, France, and Spain and the effects they had on the art that was produced in those countries.

3. Discuss the development of architecture in Italy from the 15$^{th}$ through the 17$^{th}$ centuries. Select one architect from each century that you think best exemplifies the architecture of the Early Renaissance, the High Renaissance and the Baroque period, and discuss how the styles of each period are embodied in a specific building they created.

PREPARING FOR YOUR EXAMINATIONS.
As you prepare to take your examination you should review the notes you took
on your lectures as well as the work you did in your Study Guide.   (Look back
at the **Introduction to the Study Guide** for tips on taking notes and creating
your own charts, as well as detailed instructions on studying for and taking
examinations.) If you have not yet filled out the Summary charts in the Guide,
this is the time to do it, integrating materials from your lecture notes with
materials in the Guide itself. This activity is the most useful thing that you can
do.

The self-quiz included below as well as the materials included in the **ArtStudy**
CD and the **Companion Site** for the textbook
http://art.wadsworth.com/gardnerwestern12 can be a great help in preparing
you for course examinations. The quiz below includes types of questions often
asked in art history exam examinations: multiple choice, short answer questions,
chronology exercises, essay questions and attribution of unknown images. So
take the self-quiz and check your answers in the back of the book so that you can
see how well you grasp the material.

# Self-Quiz
# THE MODERN WORLD

**CHAPTERS 20-23**

MULTIPLE CHOICE

Circle the most appropriate answer.

1. Rococo artists most valued:

    a. disproportion and disturbed balance
    b. magnificence and order
    c. pyramidal compositions and chiaroscuro
    d. pleasure and delicacy
    e. symmetry and balance

2.  The most important Realist painter of the mid-nineteenth century was:

    a. Degas
    b. Ingres
    c. Courbet
    d. Delacroix
    e. Géricault

3. The first Impressionist exhibition was held in the year:

    a. 1825
    b. 1854
    c. 1873
    d. 1890
    e. 1910

4. The short-lived student at David's studio who soon broke with David's use of style was:

    a. Delacroix
    b. Courbet
    c. Ingres
    d. Girodet-Troison
    e. Gericault

5. The group portrait of the family of Charles IV was painted by:

    a. Ingres
    b. Goya
    c. Courbet
    d. Géricault
    e. David

6. The architect who created the Chrysler Building in the Art Déco style was:

    a. Graves
    b. Moore
    c. van Alen
    d. Wright
    e. Kahn

7. The photographer who introduced avant-garde art to the American public at his 291 Gallery in New York was:

a. Gardneer
b. Close
c. Stieglitz
d. Sheeler
e. Sherman

8. The artist who developed "combine paintings" was:

a. Oldenburg
b. Rauschenberg
c. Kelly
d. Hamilton
e. Kruger

9. Movement is an important element in much of the art of:

a. Calder
b. Smith
c. Puryear
d. Arneson
e. Hanson

10. An architect who worked primarily in the Postmodern style was:

a. Garnier
b. Gaudi
c. Graves
d. Sullivan
e. Wright

11. The famous *Horse Fair* was painted by:

a. Ingres
b. Bonheur
c. Gros
d. Kollwitz
e. Goya

12. An important sculptor who worked primarily in the Neoclassical style was:

    a. Rodin
    b. Saint-Gaudens
    c. Canova
    d. Barye
    e. Lembruck

13. The sculptor whose work was most closely associated with cubism was:

    a. Lipchitz
    b. Rodin
    c. Tinguely
    d. Giacommeti
    e. Moore

14. The architect most closely associated with the Art Nouveau movement was:

    a. Wright
    b. Gaudi
    c. van Alen
    d. Mies van der Rohe
    e. Gropius

15. Strong Expressionist tendencies are seen in the work of:

    a. Mondrian
    b. Munch
    c. Seurat
    d. Cézanne
    e. Matisse

16. The artist who believed that "the art of painting can consist only in the representation of objects visible and tangible to the painter" was:

    a. Ingres
    b. Delacroix
    c. Goya
    d. Courbet
    e. Dalí

17. The concern with images deriving directly from the subconscious is most apparent in
the work of the:

    a. Expressionists
    b. Impressionists
    c. Cubists
    d. Surrealists
    e. Post-painterly Abstractionists

18. The mural entitled *Guernica* was painted by:

    a. Braque
    b. Picasso
    c. Kollwitz
    d. Kandinsky
    e. Beckmann

19. The first exhibition of the Fauves took place in:

    a. 1850
    b. 1874
    c. 1905
    d. 1930
    e. 1948

20. The *Monument to the Third International* was designed by:

    a. Rauschenberg
    b. Ernst
    c. Tatlin
    d. Kandinsky
    e. Arp

21. Line is stressed over color in the works of:

    a. Ingres
    b. Delacroix
    c. Turner
    d. Monet
    e. Pissarro

22. Color is one of the most important factors in the work of:

   a. Braque
   b. Gabo
   c. Hannah Höch
   d. Boccioni
   e. Joseph Albers

23. Which artist uses a formal approach to painting that is closest to that of Mondrian?

   a. Friedrich
   b. Rubens
   c. Vermeer
   d. Delacroix
   e. Turner

24. Which of the following artists has the least Romantic or Expressionist approach to
    landscape painting?

   a. Friedrich
   b. Van Ruisdael
   c. Turner
   d. Cézanne
   e. Van Gogh

25. The artist <u>most</u> representative of the Impressionist style was:

   a. Van Gogh
   b. Monet
   c. Manet
   d. Toulouse-Lautrec
   e. Munch

26. Which of the following is a court style developed as a reaction against the formality
    of Louis XIV and characterized by a light and delicate treatment of sensual
    subjects?

   a. Neoclassicism
   b. Rococo
   c. Classical Baroque
   d. Romanticism
   e. Impressionism

27. The Spanish painter who most effectively combined realism and fantasy was:

    a. Velásquez
    b. Zurabran
    c. Goya
    d. Miró
    e. Ribera

28. The sculptor who effectively combined aspects of Impressionism, Romanticism, and Expressionism in his work was:

    a. Canova
    b. Calder
    c. Maillol
    d. Rodin
    e. Lembruck

29. The Post-Impressionist who based his work on the color theories of Delacroix and the scientists Helmholtz and Chevreul was:

    a. Van Gogh
    b. Gauguin
    c. Cézanne
    d. Seurat
    e. Toulouse-Lautrec

30. The artist who did many self-portraits in a Surrealist style was:

    a. Géricault
    b. Kahlo
    c. Man Ray
    d. Ernst
    e. Chicago

31. The harsh, flat lighting and the juxtaposition of a nude woman with two men dressed in contemporary clothes shocked the public when Manet first exhibited his famous work entitled:

    a. *Le Déjeuner sur l'Herbe*
    b. *Le Moulin de la Galette*
    c. *A Sunday on La Grande Jatte*
    d. *The Spirit of the Dead Watching*
    e. *The Night Café*

32. Which of the following artists was famous for his photographic studies of motion?

    a. Gardner
    b. Sheeler
    c. Hopper
    d. Muybridge
    e. Stieglitz

33. An important video artist is:

    a. Paik
    b. Bell
    c. Beuys
    d. Christo
    e. Shapiro

34. The landscape painter who influenced Delacroix and anticipated both the attitude and technique of Impressionism was:

    a. Turner
    b. Constable
    c. Friedrich
    d. Van Ruisdael
    e. Courbet

35. A large construction of Earth Art, called Spiral Jetty, was designed by:

    a. Smith
    b. Hesse
    c. Hockney
    d. Abakanowicz
    e. Smithson

36. Which of the following styles best describes the work of Baron Gros?

    a. Impressionist
    b. Romantic
    c. Neoclassic
    d. Realist
    e. Symbolist

37. Which of the following styles best describes the work of Canova?

    a. Impressionist
    b. Romantic
    c. Neoclassic
    d. Realist
    e. Symbolist

38. Which of the following styles best describes the work of Gustave Moreau?

    a. Impressionist
    b. Romantic
    c. Neoclassic
    d. Realist
    e. Symbolist

39. Which of the following styles best describes the work of Gauguin?

    a. Impressionist
    b. Post-Impressionist
    c. Expressionist
    d. Realist
    e. Symbolist

40. Which of the following styles best describes the work of Bierstadt?

    a. Impressionist
    b. Romantic
    c. Neoclassic
    d. Post-Impressionist
    e. Symbolist

41. Which of the following styles best describes the work of Eakins?

    a. Impressionist
    b. Romantic
    c. Neoclassic
    d. Realist
    e. Symbolist

42. Which of the following styles best describes the work of Monet?
    a. Impressionist
    b. Expressionist
    c. Art Nouveau
    d. Realist
    e. Symbolist

43. Which of the following styles best describes the work of Odilon Redon?

    a. Impressionist
    b. Romantic
    c. Neoclassic
    d. Realist
    e. Symbolist

44. Which of the following styles best describes the work of Rivera?

    a. Cubism
    b. Fauvism
    c. Surrealism
    d. Constructivism
    e. Mexican Muralist

45. Which of the following styles best describes the work of Matisse?

    a. Cubism
    b. Fauvism
    c. Surrealism
    d. Constructivism
    e. Futurism

46. Which of the following styles best describes the work of Naum Gabo?

    a. Cubism
    b. Dada
    c. Surrealism
    d. Constructivism
    e. Abstract Expressionism

47. Which of the following styles best describes the work of Jackson Pollock?

    a. Cubism
    b. Fauvism
    c. Abstract Expressionism
    d. Mexican Muralist
    e. Futurism

48. Which of the following styles best describes the work of Lichtenstein?

    a. Cubism
    b. Dada
    c. Pop art
    d. Constructivism
    e. Abstract Expressionism

49. Which of the following styles best describes the work of Magritte?

    a. Cubism
    b. Dada
    c. Surrealism
    d. Constructivism
    e. Abstract Expressionism

50. The Crystal Palace, London was designed by:

    a. Portman
    b. Gaudi
    c. Wright
    d. Paxton
    e. Gehry

51. Portland Building, Oregon was designed by:

    a. Portman
    b. Gaudi
    c. Wright
    d. Paxton
    e. Graves

52. Bauhaus, Dessau, was designed by:

    a. Portman
    b. Gropius
    c. Wright
    d. Paxton
    e. Gehry

53. Pompadou Center, Paris, was designed by:

    a. Portman
    b. Gaudi
    c. Mies van der Rohe
    d. Rogers and Piano
    e. Gehry

54. The Guggenheim Museum in Bilbao was designed by:

    a. Portman
    b. Le Corbusier
    c. Wright
    d. Paxton
    e. Gehry

55. Schroder House, Utrecht was designed by:

    a. Reitveld
    b. Gaudi
    c. Mies van der Rohe
    d. Paxton
    e. Saarinin

56. Monticello in Virginia was designed by:

    a. Mies van der Rohe
    b. Gaudi
    c. Richardson
    d. Jefferson
    e. Saarinen

57. Notre Dame du Haut, Ronchamp, was designed by:

    a. Le Corbusier
    b. Gaudi
    c. Richardson
    d. Paxton
    e. Rogers and Piano

58.  The Marshall Field wholesale store in Chicago was designed by:

    a. Portman
    b. Gaudi
    c. Richardson
    d. Paxton
    e. Saarinin


## SHORT ANSWER QUESTIONS

Answer the question or finish the sentence.

59. Name two Surrealist painters:

60. What was the significance of the Armory show?

61. What did Richard Boyle, Robert Adam, and John Wood have in common?

62. In what type of painting did Vigée-Lebrun specialize?

63. List a Minimalist sculptor and briefly describe the style.

64. Who designed the Vietnam Memorial in Washington DC?

65. Who was the leader of Neoclassicism in 19th-century France?

66. What was the political significance of Géricault's *Raft of the Medusa*?

67. Who was William Blake?

68. Name three artists who worked for Napoleon:

69. What type of lighting was preferred by Joseph Wright of Derby?

70. Name the English painter who was famous for his satirical scenes of social criticism:

71. What was the political meaning attributed to David's *Oath of the Horatii*?

72. What was the Hudson River school? Name one artist associated with it.

73. Which artistic style created vibrant effects of light through juxtaposition of bits of pure color?

74. Name four artists who are known as Post-Impressonists:

75. What was the major significance of the materials and structural techniques used by Joseph Paxton in the Crystal Palace?

76. Name the artist who blended Cubist form and Fauvist color with memories of his home village:

77. Name the artist who designed a series of giant monuments based on simple everyday objects:

78. What was the significance of the Bauhaus and name three artists, designers or architects who were associated with it?

79. What is meant by "Deconstructionist" architecture?

80. Name three 20th-century female artists who use art as a political weapon:

81. What was the political significance of Picasso's *Guernica*?

82. Name three European artists who emigrated to the United States in the 1930s and 1940s and influenced American artists.

83. Compare the two sculptures below, attributing each to an artist, country, and decade. Give the reasons for your attributions.

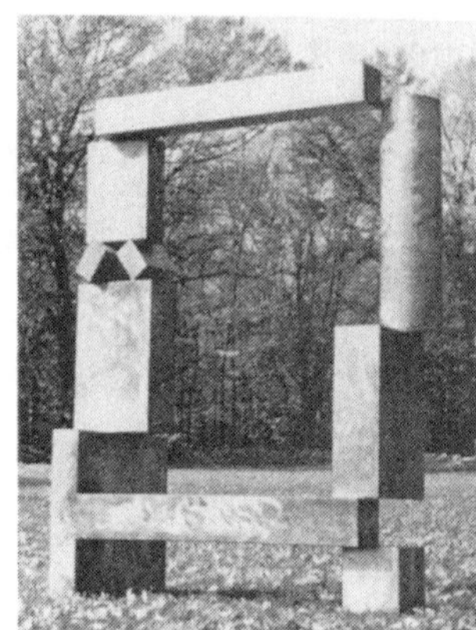

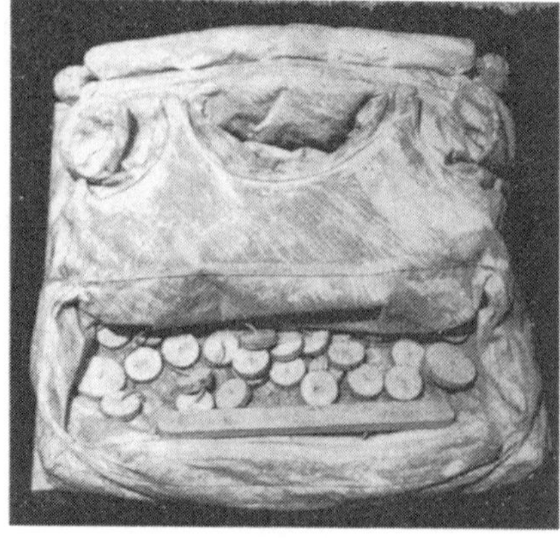

A. Artist

Country:

Decade:

Reason:

B. Artist

Country:

Decade:

Reason:

84. Compare the two sculptural groups below, attributing each to an artist, country, approximate date, and style. Give the reasons for your attributions.

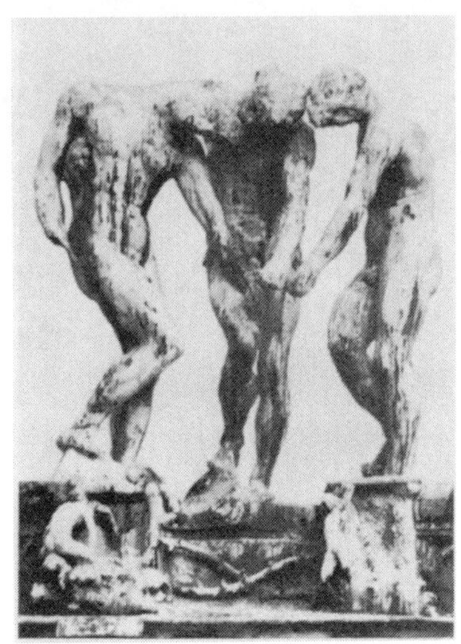

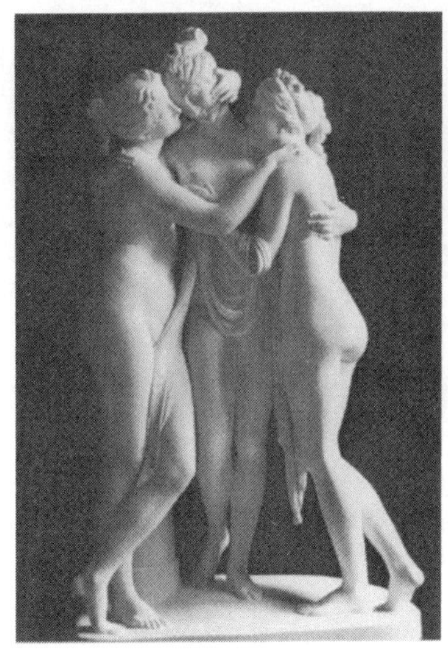

A. Artist

Country:

Decade:

Reason:

B. Artist

Country:

Decade:

Reason:

85. Compare the two abstractions below, attributing each to an artist and approximate date. Give the reasons for your attributions.

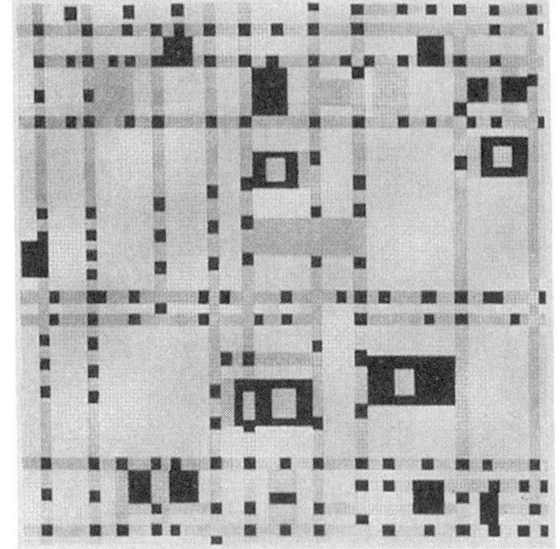

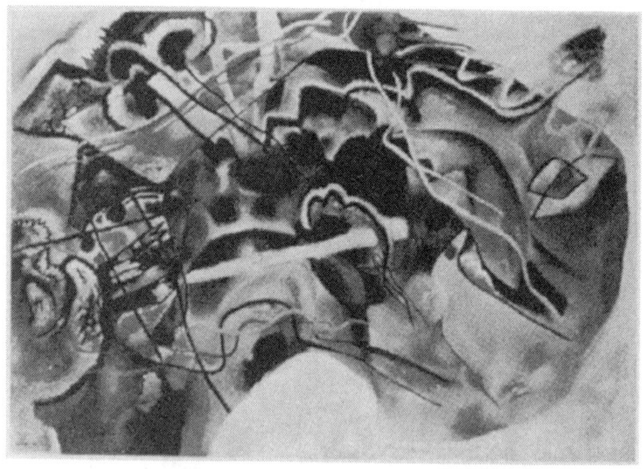

A. Artist

Country:

Decade:

Reason:

B. Artist

Country:

Decade:

Reason:

86. Compare the two landscapes below, attributing each to an artist and approximate date. Give the reasons for your attributions

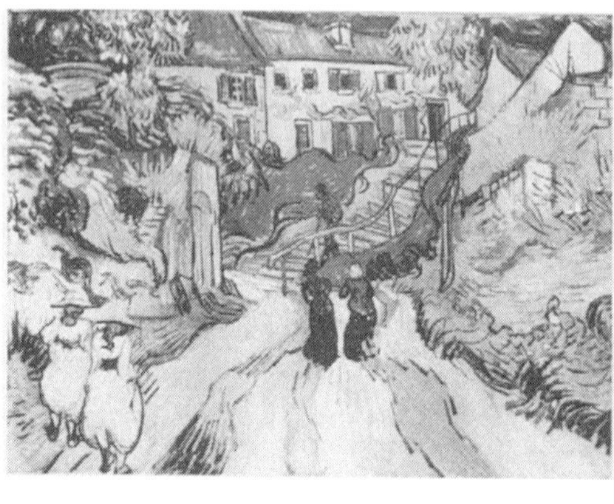

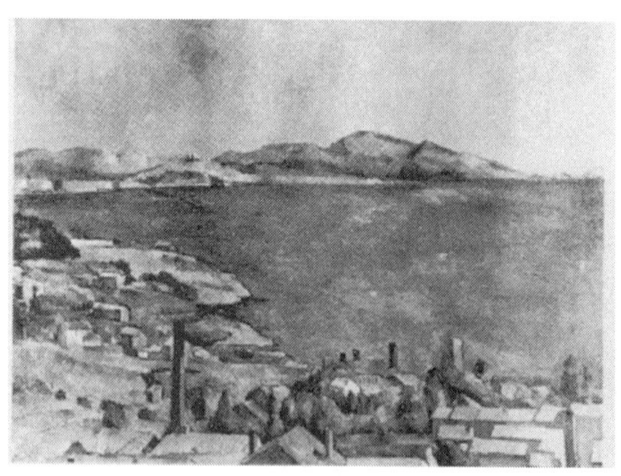

A. Artist

Date:

Reason:

B. Artist

Date:

Reason:

87. The two paintings reproduced here reflect very different ways of depicting a still life. Attribute each to an artist, a style or stylistic grouping, and a decade. Give the reasons for your attributions. What do you think were the major concerns of each artist?

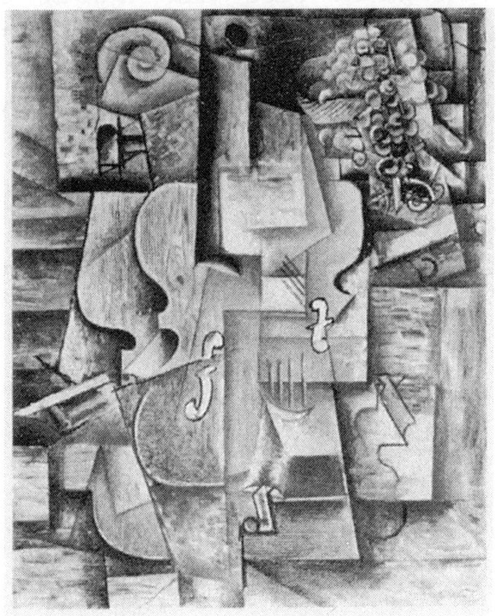 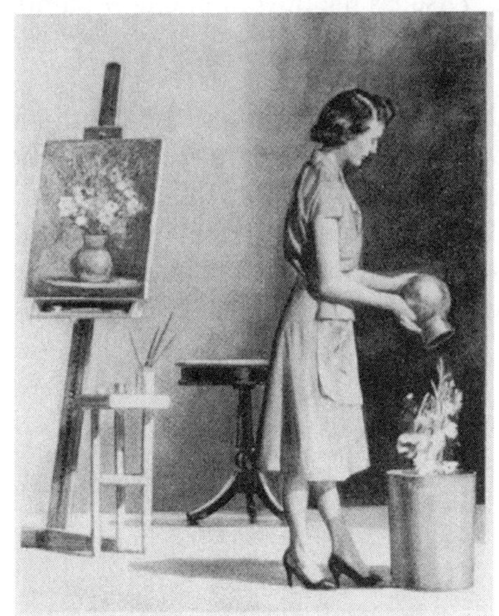

A. Artist

Style:

Decade:

Reason:

B. Artist

Style:

Decade:

Reason:

ESSAYS

Select one essay, and be sure and cite specific examples to illustrate your argument.

1. Discuss the development of painting in America in the second half of the 20th century. What did it adopt from European avant-garde artists, and what was uniquely American?

2. Compare 20th-century International Style architecture with so-called "deconstruction" architecture. What are the basic principles of each, and how do they differ?

3. Discuss the development of Neoclassicism and Romanticism in Europe in the 18th and 19th centuries.  What characteristics can be identified with each style? Discuss specific works that illustrate these characteristics.

MULTIPLE CHOICE; CHRONOLOGY AND STYLE

| | | | | |
|---|---|---|---|---|
| 1. b | 11. a | 21. d | 31. c | 41. e |
| 2. c | 12. d | 22. b | 32. b | 42. b |
| 3. a | 13. c | 23. b | 33. b | 43. c |
| 4. d | 14. b | 24. c | 34. d | 44. a |
| 5. b | 15. b | 25. e | 35. d | 45. e |
| 6. d | 16. c | 26. e | 36. b | 46. a |
| 7. d | 17. a | 27. d | 37. e | 47. b |
| 8. c | 18. b | 28. b | 38. d | 48. d |
| 9. e | 19. c | 29. c | 39. c | 49. e |
| 10. a | 20. c | 30. e | 40. d | 50. e |

GEOGRAPHIC EXERCISE

51. Michelangelo, Italy

52. Balthasar Neuman, Germany

53. Jan Van Eyck, Flanders (Netherlands)

54. Brunellesci, Italy

55. Inigo Jones, England (Great Britain)

56. Borromini, Italy

57. Grunewald, Germany

58. Bernini, Italy

59. Michelangelo, Italy

60. Le Brune and/or Hardouin-Mansart, France

SHORT ANSWERS

61. The "Maniera Greca," also known as the Italo-Byzantine style, is characterized by a gold background, flattened figures, and shallow "stage-set" space.

62. El Greco worked primarily in Spain, and the majority of his pictures had religious subject matter.

63. In Good Government Lorenzetti showed the peaceful life in the city and country, as well as allegorical figures. In addition he did scenes illustrating Bad Government. The everyday scenes from the county and city were innovative.

64. Three from the following: Masaccio, Brunelleschi, Uccello, Ghierti, Piero della Francesca, and Mantegna.

65. Ghirlandaio was a synthesizer, not an innovator. His work presents an excellent picture of Florence at the end of the fifteenth century, giving detailed representations of the life, pageantry, costume and material wealth of the citizens.

66. The Medici.

67. Artists using aerial perspective lessen the intensity of colors and blur the edges of forms to indicate distance. They often use blue tones that recede to indicate far distance. Linear perspective is a mathematically based system that creates a window into space, and in which all parallel lines that are perpendicular to the picture plane converge at a single point known as the vanishing point, which falls on the horizon.

68. Jean Goujon created elegantly elongated and graceful figures in the Mannerist style.

69. Cranach was a friend of Martin Luther who was responsible for starting the Protest Reformation in Germany. Cranch created woodcuts praising the protestant cause and criticizing the papacy.

70. Van der Weyden stressed human action and emotion rather than the complex symbolism and precise rendering seen in van Eyck's work.

71. Portraiture, much of which was done in England.

72. Four of the following: Bramante, Michelangelo, della Porta, Maderno, Bernini.

73. Still life

74. Phillip IV of Spain

75. Dynamic composition, use of tenebroso or "night lighting" that utilized strong contrasts of light and dark and realistic detail.

76. Artists working in the Grand Manner selected grand heroic or religious subjects not low life subjects of genre scenes, and their works were painted broadly, without attention to minute details.

77. Any of the following: East façade of the Louvre, Versailles Palace, the Orleans wing of the Chateau of Blois, the Church of the Invalides in Paris.

78. Bernini

79. Characteristic scenes of a city, best exemplified in the work of Canalletto.

80. Two from: Inigo Jones, Wren, and Vanburgh.


IDENTIFICATION:

81.  A. Jan van Eyck, Flanders, fifteenth century, Northern Renaissance (*The Annunciation*, c. 1435. National Gallery, Washington, D.C.)
     B. Raphael, Italy, sixteenth century, High Renaissance (*La Belle Jardiniére*, 1507-1508. Louvre, Paris).
     The precision and clarity of the rendition of every form in this Annunciation scene indicate its fifteenth-century northern origin. The emphasis on the specific, as shown in the rich brocaded robe and the sparkling jewels, point to van Eyck as the artist. Similar details are shown in the *Ghent Altarpiece*. For example, the slightly awkward position of the Virgin of this panel is very similar to that of the Virgin on the exterior of his *Ghent Altarpiece*. The slight upward tilt of the floor indicates that single-point linear perspective was not used to construct the architectural setting, as most likely would have been done by an Italian painter of the same period. Rich surface, precise details, and symbolism are more important than unified space. As in other fifteenth-century Netherlandish works, disguised symbolism plays an important role in this painting, with such things as the scenes depicted on the capitals of the columns and the tiles of the floor adding to the devotional meaning of the altarpiece.
     *The Madonna with the Christ Child and St. John* is an excellent example of Raphael's High Renaissance style, for it demonstrates the tightly organized pyramidal composition that was favored by High Renaissance artists, as well as the subtle chiaroscuro Raphael used to model the idealized faces. Like the *Madonna of the Meadow*, this work demonstrates Raphael's striving to combine grace, dignity, and idealism with simplicity and logic. The beauty and calm dignity of these figures and their monumental form illustrate Raphael's great achievement in merging Christian devotion with pagan beauty.

82. Bernini, seventeenth century, Italy, Baroque (Sant'Andrea al Quirihnale, Rome, 1658-1670.)
     The building illustrated here very clearly demonstrates the approach to form favored by Baroque architects. Variations of the oval were much more popular with Baroque architects than variations of the square and circle, which were the ideal forms for Renaissance architects. That preference is apparent in the plan of the Baroque church shown here. The façade also demonstrates the distinctive approach of Baroque architects. While the typical renaissance façade is composed of discrete geometric units, carefully proportioned and coordinated, the façade of Sant'Andrea is composed of forms molded deeply in space, with curve playing against curve, creating a rich plastic surface. Many of the stylistic characteristics of this church, which was designed by Bernini, are apparent in other Baroque buildings as well, for example Borromini's church of San Carlo alle Quattro Fontane, Guarini's Palazzo Carignano, and the piazza of Saint Peter's, which was also designed by Bernini. All share with this building the Baroque delight in dynamic forms that reach out and embrace space, plastic handling of surfaces, contrast of concave

and convex forms, and preference for oval plans rather than the more static forms of circle and square.


83. A. Holland, seventeenth century (Philips Koninck, *Landscape with a Hawking Party*, National Gallery, London.)

B. Italy, seventeenth century (Pietro da Cortona, *Triumph of Barberini*, 1633-1639. Ceiling fresco. Gran Salone, Palazzo Barberini, Rome.)

These Baroque paintings share the seventeenth-century's expansiveness and dynamism. Like Baroque scientists, the artists of these works see physical nature as matter in motion through space and time. However, while the Dutch artist paints the motion of clouds through a realistic landscape, dappled with a constantly changing light, the Italian artist gives an intense physical reality to his personifications of abstract ideas and then sets his massive figures into dynamic motion.

The differences between the paintings can be attributed in part to the desires and expectations of the patrons. The Italian artist was commissioned to paint an allegorical painting in praise of his powerful ecclesiastical patron and used a form similar to that used by Pozzo in his *Glorification of St. Ignatius*, painted on the ceiling of one of the huge new Roman churches. The Dutch artist, on the other hand, was working for the open market, attempting to paint something that would be appreciated and purchased by a prosperous Dutch burgher to decorate his residence. These patrons were not interested in allegory, but rather in something real, such as the portrayal of the changing moods of their beloved skies. The Dutch Protestant preferred to worship God reflected in his works, rather than under the majestic painted ceilings so popular in Catholic Rome.


84. A. Rembrandt, Holland, seventeenth century (Aristotle with the Bust of Homer, 1653. Metropolitan Museum of Art, New York.)

B. Vermeer, Holland, seventeenth century (Girl Reading a Letter, c. 1655-1660. Staatliche Kunstsammlungen, Dresden.)

Rembrandt and Vermeer shared with other seventeenth-century Dutch artists an intense interest in the optics of light. However, their handling of it was quite different. Vermeer was primarily concerned with the creation of pictoral illusion and with extremely subtle optical effects. His attention to the effects of a warm and sunny light entering a quiet room, its reflections on the glass and the varying textures it illuminates are very clearly seen in this painting.

Rembrandt, on the other hand, used subtle modulations of light and dark to indicate spiritual or psychic states, to explore nuances of character and mood. The man represented here shares with many of the others portrayed by Rembrandt a sense of inwardness, of quiet contemplation. Only a portion of his face emerges out of the darkness, while the bust, on which he rests his hand, seems to glow with light. Rembrandt makes us wonder about the relationship between the man and the bust, even if we do not know that they represent Aristotle, the famous philosopher, contemplating a bust of the blind poet Homer. Is he recognizing the superiority of Homer's intuitive wisdom over his own more worldly knowledge and success, symbolized by the golden chain? (Even if you didn't write anything about the subject Rembrandt was representing, I hope that you wrote something about the mysterious effects he created.)

85. A. Michelangelo, Italy, seventeenth century, High Renaissance (*The Bearded Giant*, 1530-1533. Galleria dell' Accademia, Florence.)

B. Bernini, Italy, seventeenth century, Baroque (*Rape of Proserpine*, 1621-1622. Borghese Gallery Rome.)

These two works are typical of the sculptural styles of Michelangelo and Bernini. While some of Michelangelo's works shared the qualities found in the work of other High Renaissance artists, this work demonstrates the quality of "terribilita" so characteristic of his personal style. Pent-up passion and power are represented here rather than calm and ideal beauty. This figure has an even more massive physique than the *Bound Slave* illustrated in the text, but like it, it seems to represent the human soul struggling to free itself from matter. While the action of Michelangelo's figure can be understood from a single view—as is typical of most Renaissance sculpture—one must walk around the Bernini group in order to fully appreciate the complex composition, a characteristic of much Baroque sculpture. As he did in his rendition of David, Bernini captures the split-second action of the most dramatic moment. The two struggling bodies pull against each other with great energy, and Bernini contrasts the strong musculature of the male figure with the softer quality of female flesh. Virtuoso treatment of surface textures, combined with great energy and movement, is typical of Bernini, as is the work's expansive quality as it reaches out into space and refuses to be confined to the block from which it is carved.


ESSAYS:
Answers found throughout the text.

MULTIPLE CHOICE

| | | | | | |
|---|---|---|---|---|---|
| 1. d | 11. b | 21. a | 31. a | 41. d | 51. e |
| 2. c | 12. c | 22. e | 32. d | 42. a | 52. b |
| 3. c | 13. a | 23. c | 33. a | 43. e | 53. d |
| 4. c | 14. b | 24. d | 34. a | 44. e | 54. e |
| 5. d | 15. b | 25. b | 35. a | 45. d | 55. a |
| 6. c | 16. d | 26. b | 36. b | 46. d | 56. d |
| 7. c | 17. d | 27. c | 37. c | 47. c | 57.a |
| 8. b | 18. b | 28. d | 38. e | 48.c | 58. c |
| 9. a | 19. c | 29. d | 39. b | 49.c | |
| 10.c | 20. c | 30. b | 40.b | 50. d | |

SHORT ANSWERS

59. Two from Dali, Magritte, Ernst, and Miro.

60. The Armory show introduced America to avant-garde European art.

61. All three were eighteenth-century British architects.

62. Portraiture

63. Tony Smith and/or Donald Judd (Maya Lin could be considered a Minimalist as well). They created three-dimensional objects, often in primary geometric forms, that often lack identifiable subjects, colors, surface textures and narrative elements.

64. Maya Lin

65. Ingres

66. Géricault's *Raft of the Medusa* was critical of the government in that it portrayed an incident in which the crew of a passenger ship abandoned the passengers after a wreck, leaving them to fend for themselves.

67. An eighteenth-century British visionary poet and painter.

68. David, Canova, Gros, and Vignon

69. Dramatic lighting resembling Caravaggio's tenebroso, often produced by candlelight or moonlight.

70. Hogarth

71. It was considered a call to arms and a call to sacrifice for the republic as the Horatii had done.

72. A group of nineteenth-century American landscape painters who worked in the
eastern United States along the Hudson River.  Thomas Cole was one of them.

73. Impressionism

74. Cezanne, Seurat, van Gogh, Gauguin, or Toulouse-Lautrec

75. Paxton used structural elements honestly for what they were and did not give them
revival-style decoration.  In addition, he used prefabricated parts that allowed rapid
construction. His iron supports were steps on the way to twentieth-century skyscraper
construction.

76. Chagall

77. Oldenburg

78. The Bauhus, founded in 1919, was dedicated to training artists, designers, and
architects to meet twentieth century needs.  The teachers at the Bauhaus made no
distinction between artists and craftsmen.  They stressed simplicity and elegance as
well as functional design, and influenced twentieth century design world-wide.
Gropius and later Mies van der Rohe served as director, and among the artists and
designers who taught there were Moholy-Nagy,  Kandinsky,  Klee,  Albers, Breuer
and Stölzl.

79. Deconstructionist architects attempt to disorient observers by disrupting conventional
categories of architecture using haphazard mixture of forms.

80. Any three from Judy Chicago, Miriam Schapiro, Cindy Sherman, Barbara Kruger,
Ana Mendieta, Hannah Wilke, Kiki Smith, Faith Ringold, Adrian Piper, and Lorna
Simpson.

81. Picasso portrayed the horrors of the bombing of the small Spanish town of Guernica
by the Nazis at the beginning of the Spanish Civil War.

82. Any three from Beckmann, Grosz, Gropius, Moholy- Nagy, Algers, Breuer, Mies van
der Rohe, Ernst, Dali, Eton, Leger and Lipchitz.


IDENTIFICATION

83. A. David Smith, United States, 1960s (*Cubi XXVII*, 1965, Guggenheim Museum,
New York.)
     B. Claes Oldenburg, United States, 1960s (*Model Ghost Typewriter,* 1963. Sidney
Janis Gallery, New York.)
          Both of these pieces of sculpture were created by American artists in the 1960s,
and they represent two very different approaches to art. Smith is representative of the

Formalist/Structuralist approach, which aims to eliminate the human element in art in favor of formal machinelike perfection. Like the steel sculpture by Smith illustrated in the text (another *Cubi*), this one shows his interest in arranging "solid, geometric masses in remarkable equilibriums of strength and buoyancy." Notice particularly the precarious balance of the columnar form on the upper right part of the sculpture. The beautifully machined surfaces of the forms demonstrate Smith's interest in contemporary machines and his professed desire to turn his studio into a factory.

Oldenburg's approach is almost diametrically opposed, for one of his goals was to humanize the machine, which he does with a kind of sly humor by means of his "soft" sculptures. The various mechanisms of the soft typewriter sag and assume a strangely grotesque organic quality, which completely denies its function as a machine. Oldenburg's fantasy seems to be a combination of Dada mockery of society and the interest of American Pop artists in the forms of the commercial world around them.


84. A. Rodin, France, late nineteenth to early twentieth century (*Three Fates from the Gate of Hell*, 1880-1917. Musée Rodin, Paris.)

B. Canova, Italy or France, early nineteenth century, Neoclassicism (*Three Graces*, 1814. Ny Carlsburg Glyptych, Copenhagen.)

These two sculptured groups demonstrate the difference between Canova's cool and formal Neoclassicism and Rodin's much more emotional style, which combines elements from Romanticism, Impressionism, and an expressive Realism. Rodin's figures are cast in bronze from clay models, and his use of soft clay enabled him to create subtle variations and shifts of the places under the play of light and thus to achieve effects that were impossible to an artist like Canova, who carved directly into marble. Rodin's fluid modeling is analogous to the deft Impressionist brush stroke, but the exaggerations of the forms and the striking gestures of the three figures as they point downward echo the dramatic intensity of Romantic and Expressionist works. The impression of work in-progress created by the figures seems to derive from the unfinished works of Michelangelo, which influenced Rodin deeply. Rodin's concern with dramatic statement and with expressive bodily pose and gesture shows clearly the influence of Michelangelo.

Canova's graceful female figures derive from very different sources. There is a lingering Rococo charm, but the precise technique used to create the idealized figures, which combine careful detailing and generalized forms, is clearly in the Classical tradition. These three figures are closely related to Coanova's representation of Pauline Borghese as Venus, for they demonstrate the same type of femininity" ideal and seemingly distant, yet human and accessible at the same time.


85. A. Mondrian, second-quarter twentieth century (*Broadway Boogie Woogie*, 1942-1943. Museum of Modern Art, New York.)

B. Kandinsky, first-quarter twentieth century (*Picture with a White Edge*, 1913. Guggenheim Museum, New York.)

These two compositions illustrate the range of experimentation that was found in the development of abstract art in the early twentieth century. Mondrian's composition, like the one illustrated in the text, is composed exclusively of straight lines that form squares and rectangles of various sizes, arranged very carefully on a two-dimensional surface to create a subtle asymmetrical balance. He was interested in the idea of an absolute artistic order, but he did not want mechanical uniformity. This composition illustrates his belief that "true reality is attained through dynamic movement in equilibrium," for while there is a sense of balance in the composition, there is no symmetry, and the shapes of the rectangles are infinitely varied. Yet, he is not unlike the Neoclassical artists, since his approach, like theirs, can best be described as deliberate and studious.

Although the words used to describe the Romantic artist as "impetuous, improvisational, and distinctive" are out if place in describing Mondrian's work, they do seem to describe exactly the approach used by Kandinsky in the works illustrated here and in the text. The painting demonstrates the point at which Kandinsky's exploration of the motional and psychological properties of color, line, and shape have dispensed with the depiction of subject matter and have moved into the realm of pure abstraction. The title, which he used for many of the pictures of this time, including *Improvisation 28* in the text, aptly describes his approach and is very different from the deliberate, intellectual one of Mondrian, Where Mondrian's lines are vertical or horizontal, lines of masses and color move across Kandinsky's canvas in all directions, movements and arrangements that seem to burst directly from his subconscious. Kandinsky's own writing stresses the importance of allowing the instinctual world of the subconscious to emerge and to control directly the artistic expression of the artist. In this work we see the results of that technique.

86. A. Van Gogh, late nineteenth century (*Stairway at Auvers*, 1890. City Art Museum, St. Louis.)
 B. Cézanne, late nineteenth century (*The Gulf of Marseilles Seen from L'Estaque*, 1884-1886. Metropolitan Museum of Art, New York.)
 These two paintings, done in late nineteenth-century France by two Post-Impressionists, show the same contrast in approach that we saw in the twentieth century between Mondrian and Kandinsky. Van Gogh's approach to the painting is instinctive and emotional, while Cézanne's is deliberate and intellectual. The van Gogh landscape shows the same type of swirling, impulsive brush strokes that he used in *Starry Night*. There are no stable forms; rather everything seems to be in motion. Unfortunately, the black-and-white reproduction does not show the intense color that van Gogh loved and made such an important part of his painterly expression.
 Color was important to Cézanne too, but he used it to build up form and pictorial structure and not to express emotional states as did van Gogh. The carefully interlocked planes he developed in his painting of Mont. Sainte-Victoire are also used here and interlock forcibly on the two-dimensional surface of the canvas. As in his other landscapes, he has immobilized the shifting colors of Impressionism and has created a series of clearly defined places. This is a much more stable-looking landscape than the one created by van Gogh. Like Mondrian, Cézanne has achieved this stability by emphasizing vertical and horizontal lines in his composition, while van Gogh, like Delacroix and Kandinsky, has created an emotional and constantly changing effect in his by using diagonal lines that undulate.

87. A. Picasso or Braque, Analytic Cubism, 1910s (Picasso, *Violin and Grapes*, 1912. Museum of Modern Art, New York.)

B. Mark Tansey, Postmodernist, 1980s (*Still Life*, 1982. Metropolitan Museum of Art, New York.)

The subject of painting A, which seems to be some sort of stringed instrument and a fruit resembling grapes, is not depicted according to our usual view, but rather is dissected, spread out across the picture place, and compressed into a very shallow space. Shortly before 1910, Picasso and Braque began experimenting with ways to present the total reality of three-dimensional objects on a two-dimensional plane. They utilized multiple angles of vision and simultaneous presentations of discontinuous places to represent various aspects of their subjects. Color was kept to a minimum in these works, and the surface was broken up as forms were subjected to careful analysis. All of these characteristics are seen in the painting reproduced here, although the color range is impossible to detect in black-and-white.

Painting B shows us a traditional still life, but it is a painting within a painting. The style is a kind of careful realism like that used by a number of artists during the 1930s, but the pun is in the spirit of the work done by Mark Tansey in the 1980s. It is a kind of modern *momento mori*, not only for the flowers. Which die while their painted representation lives on, but also for the painting style of so many artists of an earlier era. Although Tansey painted many of his images in the tones of gray of a news photograph in order to create and additional level of reality, this black-and-white reproduction does not allow us to detect the color used in this still-life painting. Both Picasso and Tansey set problems for the viewer to solve: Picasso's is the analysis of pictoral space, while Tansey's concern is with a wry dissection and analysis of the convention of art and of the art world itself.

ESSAYS:
Answers found throughout the text.